- 4 AUG 2025

York St John
Library and Information Services

Please return this item on or before the due date stamped below (if using the self issue option users may write in the date themselves), **If recalled the loan is reduced to 10 days.**

RETURNED 1 9 OCT 2006	RETURNED - 9 APR 2008	
RETURNED 2 5 MAR 2007		
RETURNED 0 3 MAY 2007		
RETURNED - 3 NOV 2007		
RETURNED 2 5 MAY 2008		

Fines are payable for late return

- 4 AUG 2025

WITHDRAWN

Offside Racism
Playing the White Man

Colin King

Oxford • New York

English edition
First published in 2004 by
Berg
Editorial offices:
First Floor, Angel Court, 81 St Clements Street, Oxford OX4 1AW, UK
175 Fifth Avenue, New York, NY 10010, USA

© Colin King 2004

Berg is the imprint of Oxford International Publishers Ltd.

Library of Congress Cataloging-in-Publication data
A catalogue record for this book is available from the Library of Congress.

British Library Cataloguing-in-Publication data
A catalogue record for this book is available from the British Library.

ISBN 1 85973 724 2 (hardback)
    1 85973 729 3 (paperback)

Typeset by Avocet Typeset, Chilton, Aylesbury, Bucks
Printed in the United Kingdom by Biddles Ltd, King's Lynn.

www.bergpublishers.com

Contents

Preface

'Offside racism' 'playing the white man' is a new approach used in this book to describe the pressures placed on black and Asian people to 'act white' in order to be accepted in the twenty-first century. It focuses on the institutions of sport and the study of the cultures of soccer, to explain the barriers black players face as they seek positions as coaches and managers. It compares these experiences to those encountered on a much smaller level by Asian players entering the playing profession. The book analyses the privileges held by white men and the way they colonize the settings of soccer coaching and management that lead to different forms of racism and exclusion. It connects these forms of racism to broader social issues that have had important implications for the stereotypes made about black people inside and outside the sports context. To look more closely at the relationships between sport and society to study how exclusion operates in the institutions of soccer I use the concepts 'racialized performance' and 'racialized narrative' to show how racism can be seen in two forms. Firstly through an onside form of racism, which is made visible through the words and actions of white men, which they are often conscious of. I compared this to the offside racism, which is often implicit and which white men are not conscious of. My aim is to demonstrate that the way people inside soccer see and understand issues of race and racism leads to totally different outcomes for black, Asian and white people. 'Offside racism' 'playing the white man' is a method to explore how racism within soccer is broader than the idea of 'unwitting' prejudice as described in the Macpherson report (1999), which can more clearly analyse how institutional racism operates in football and other industries.

Acknowledgements

This book was written in memory of my brother Martin Shaw King, who died preaching the spirit and insight of an Afrocentric, and who refused to be controlled by whiteness. His energy lives on in the Martin Shaw King Trust, which inspired and supported this book. I would especially like to thank my mother, Myrtle May King, who personifies this statement from Malcolm X: 'To educate the man is to educate an individual, to educate the woman is to educate and liberate a nation.'

I would also like to thank those who took time to read this book and offered their critical feedback: Sharon Davidson, Doctor Lez Henry, Les Back, Ian King, Trevor King, Wallace Hermitt and Lorraine Marke. My profound thanks go out to my two sons Umi and Chiemeka, the future generation of writers whom I hope I have inspired.

Introduction:
Playing the Race Game in Soccer

You know when I was at Wolves as a young player I was known throughout the area as the first black player to get into the team. It was a time when people thought we couldn't tackle, we couldn't play in the cold – and then came along big, bad Darren Smith. During training one day the ball went out of play and nobody wanted to get it. And then one of the white players looks at another of the white players and laughs, saying 'Go on Darren, 'play the white man'. (Darren Smith Interview)

The above quotation from Darren Smith captures the focus of this book in microcosm. He is a member of the first generation of black players to become established within English football, and in this training session his white peers revealed something very profound about the terms on which black players are accepted. The white player urges him to 'play the white man', to act like *he* would act, to be reasonable, to go and pick the ball up out of the mud. This white player also – perhaps unwittingly – revealed that Darren was being invited to play the game according to implicitly racist rules. It is telling that this piece of racist vernacular was expressed as a 'joke'. It is often within humour that a culture reveals its deepest secrets (Basso 1979). It displays the games and acts that colonize football culture's core values. In order for Darren – or any other black player at this time – to belong and to fit in with the culture of professional soccer he has to 'play the white man' in an open, visible, onside form of racism.

This moment also shows an 'offside form of racism' as it reveals the lack of awareness from white players of the racist expectations that govern the terms on which black people enter their world of professional soccer. Black players are powerless to flag it up, as it remains unrecognized as a form of whiteness – as a structure of action – that is performed by white men who will not see or understand the long-term effects on people like Darren at the end of their playing careers. 'Playing the white man' thus can be viewed as a metaphor for the way racism operates within the world of sport. It illustrates the unseen pressures placed on black players in their relationships with white individuals inside soccer, particularly for an ex-player like Darren who was trying to make the transition from being a player to becoming a coach or manager in the late 1990s. The experiences recounted here by Darren are resonant with T. K. Utchay's (1975) prescient analysis of the culture of white colonialists in Africa. He described their behaviour through the notion of 'white manning', defined in the following way:

> 'Whitemanning' is a type of technical term used to describe one of the strangest actions in existence. It is the name for a practice introduced by the white man, by which one white man thinks himself superior to another, not for any reason such as academic qualifications or financial means, but simply because he has a white skin. It is employed to describe the conduct of certain Africans who slavishly imitate the white man and go about despising other black men for reasons they do not know, simply because the white man does so. (Utchay, 1975: 42)

Utchay draws our attention to whiteness as a *performance* that affects people on both sides of the colour line, albeit in very different ways.

Offside Racism aims to make whiteness transparent as a particular type of performance through a range of acts and narratives that are adopted by white men. These acts formed the types of assimilation that first confronted large numbers of black players in the 1980s and characterize the specifically different experiences of Asian players as they start their careers in the twenty-first century.

More significantly, the book explores experiences like Darren's by making visible the pressures that white men place on black men and, to a much smaller extent, the potential pressures on the emerging Asian players. It asserts that these are two fundamentally different groups acting out different, but complex and changing cultural histories. It considers the 'black British' phenomena as part of a longer history of contamination within English society and the English game. It examines the rules relating to racism and exclusion inside the institutions of soccer by revealing the barriers that black players face, and their responses. More crucially it connects these experiences to broader social and political issues by considering the theoretical debates that have influenced the relationships between sport, society and racism. To understand this relationship, I see embodied social action and patterns of discourse as new tools for examining how inequality take places in the spheres of the playing field, coaching, management and administration.

This book also focuses on how racism operates inside these institutions by looking at 'institutional racism' as an ineffective definition that has been used to explain racism in other organizational settings. In the Macpherson Report (1999) institutional racism is defined as:

> The collective failure of an organization to provide an appropriate, professional service to people because of their culture, colour or ethnic origins. It may be detected in processes, attitudes or behaviours that amount to discrimination through unwitting prejudices, ignorance and thoughtlessness and racist stereotyping that disadvantage racial and ethnic groups. (Macpherson, 1999: 17)

The book broadens Macpherson's (1999) definition of institutional racism to examine more specifically how its unconscious and unintended consequences are represented as actions with outcomes, and to examine particularly the loose use of the term 'unwitting'. It recognizes that all individual actions, whether 'unwitting' or not, can and do amount to a 'collective failure' and that black, Asian and white men can all be implicated. Miles (1993: 87) offers a model that will be used in this book to name the ways racism, as a complicated process of exclusion operates inside organizational cultures like soccer:

> The concept of institutional racism therefore refers to circumstances where racism is embodied in exclusionary practices or in formally non-racialised discourse. But in both cases it is necessary to demonstrate the determinate influence of racism.

Racism is a cultural process observed in institutions like football by how individuals act and how men talk as a result of different historical experiences. This book looks at how the culture of an organization reveals its 'racism' through the ways that white men create forms of familiarity that ensure that they are never made accountable for the ways they exclude predominantly black men from different spheres of the football industry. It analyses the privileges white men have and their capacity to exploit the institutions of football by the ways they develop patterns of being at ease that lead to the unconscious forms of racism that black men fail to see. In this respect I am using the 'onside racism' and 'offside racism' dichotomy to understand the way white men function that lead to different types of racism inside football. I argue that these performances of whiteness, featured through white, masculine identities, are at the very centre of the institutional cultures that influence the way that black and Asian men must act to be accepted.

Institutionalized racism inside football will be analysed using Goffman's (1956) theory of performance with Fanon's (1967) approach to racial identity to examine how 'racialized performances' operate. This link between race identity and performance shows that how men act provides a means to explore how they see and experience racism and develop their place in the social world of soccer. More critically the book examines the consequences for black and Asian players adjusting to the stereotypes made in relation to their body and to the personal changes necessary to move into the institutions of soccer. Fanon (1967: 112) illustrates the pressures placed on black men to survive in a white world, which I will examine during the course of this book in the context of soccer:

> Not only must the black man be black, he must be black in relation to the white man. In the white world the man of colour encounters powers in his bodily schema; consciousness of his body is solely a negative activity. It is a third-person consciousness. The body is surrounded by an atmosphere of certain uncertainty. He discovered his

blackness, his ethnic characteristics. Battered down by tom-toms, cannibalism, intellectual deficiency, fetishism, racial defects, slave ships.

Throughout this book I will use Fanon's (1967) work to look at the challenges faced by black men to assume the culture and the language of the white man, along with the overwhelming need to adopt the white man's standards of behaviour through the use of the 'white mask'. I will use the metaphor of the 'white mask' to show how black players moving into playing, coaching and management spaces, use it as a public performance and as an internal mechanism to survive being perceived simply as black or much later on as Asian, and who have to assimilate and be controlled by white men.

Frankenberg's (1993) idea of race cognizance is central to exploring racism as either onside, visible and conscious, or offside, invisible and unconscious to the men in soccer, and to understanding these differences. The idea of consciousness, how individuals understand their lives and the responsibility they take to see, and name and change racism inside the industry of soccer is crucial to the whole book. More specifically, in this book I will discuss the contradiction between consciousness and actions and the implications for racism inside football, which has many complex and contradictory forms. I suggest that race consciousness influences black, Asian and white men's performances and their responses to racism, particularly white men's ability to have their acts of offside racism acknowledged as onside acts, which they want to change. In this book we will see how the idea of performance can be used to analyse the social roles performed by white personnel and the different ways black and Asian men access the stages where white men construct these roles. More specifically, we will see how the idea of 'mystification' – the social distance maintained between white men and black men trying to move into their position – operates. The book looks at the notion of 'teams', exploring the 'routines' protected by white men and how they control access into their 'social establishment'. It unpicks the social establishment and illustrates the types of cultural compromises that are needed to enter the white man's team in two stages – firstly through the 'front stage' and secondly through the 'back stage'. In this book I will reveal how team performances are influenced by how white men act in the front stage, the pitch, training ground and the interface with black men, where forms of onside racism are apparent. This will be compared with how white men operate in the back stage, the implicit and unspoken offside processes of racism. The book opens up these back stages and how information about the role of the coach and manager is controlled in an industry where appointments to such positions are often informal. I explore how secrets become fundamental to how white men act to gain entry into the social establishment. The book makes transparent how white men maintain exclusivity through these secrets and how they develop character relationships with each other in which they learn different gestures and self-maintenance. It examines the types of team performances that operate in soccer and that lead to regions in which white men keep secrets from black men and inhibit their ability to become coaches and managers.

In the process of analysing how racism in football takes place I will use Portelli's (1991) work on narratives to look at the ways black, Asian and white men, through their talk, make sense of their lives inside soccer and the powers they have to survive and progress. Throughout this book I explore the types of racism black players face, focusing particularly on the psychological impact of racism described in the work of Kovell (1988) in which he describes two types, dominant and aversive. Dominant forms of racism appeal to the crude onside forms of racism by the ways that white men act towards black players in the field of play through a historical reproduction of racist physical threats, seeing the black player as an animal. Aversive form of racism will be used to examine the behaviour of white men to distance themselves from black men in the institutions of coaching and management in which they create an exclusive white male culture. The book suggests that black men can invert the pressure to act on the terms of white men, using Basso's (1979) work on the use of parody to explore how they want to 'play the white man'. Secondly and more critically, the book explores the political options available using Malcolm X's (1967) notion of the 'field nigger' and the 'house nigger'. It suggests that the strategies used to survive racism reveal that 'playing the white man' is now a much more complicated and multifaceted mechanism and not simply about selling out or having to violently defy racism.

Why the Book

In 1977 I was told I would not make it as a professional footballer as 'niggers couldn't read the game'. In 1994 I was then physically assaulted by a white course tutor whilst trying to obtain the Full License Coaching Award. With feelings of injustice, I approached Sports England to investigate the seriousness and extent of such experiences in relation to other black players becoming coaches and managers and the connection with black people's experiences in other institutions. I was concerned with the way the white European mind superimposes on the black African body a one-dimensional status that views it as unable to operate on any mental level. This view of the pathology of the black mind is crucial for understanding how racism operates and leads to the manifestation of exclusion featured in the relationship between sport and society. This fixed positioning of the limited ability of black people was further reinforced when told by certain white academics that I was too angry, too radical, too close, too black and ultimately not intelligent enough to research these issues. During this process I had been misdiagnosed with schizophrenia and diagnosed with dyslexia, and this motivated a determined spirit to write a book to challenge the patterns in which white men in authority seduce black people to internalize their image of incompetence and then claim they 'lack aspiration' to read the game and to write intellectually. This phenomenon is not specific to sport and the structures of football but is endemic in other organizations I have personally experienced – in education, social welfare and through the research process. This book was thus inspired by these experiences and the barriers that black people in general face in terms of being judged in their efforts to work in an environment that is dominated by white men's perceptions.

Twelve years after my experience of being called a 'nigger', my brother died and the Martin Shaw King Trust was set up in his name. The Trust aims to confront and change processes and procedures that militate against equity in the arena of our national game.

The ethos of the Trust enabled me to research and test my theory that racism and exclusion were presented through performance and narrative in the professional cultures of sport. During my corresponding Ph.D. study I critically examined the racial breakdown of professional soccer players who were making the transition into positions as coaches, managers and administrators within the current football structures from the 1980s to the start of the twenty-first century. The search revealed a clear race disparity in that the significant posts within the Premier League, the Football Association, the League Managers' Association and the Professional Footballers' Association were all held predominately by white men. Spending months telephoning football clubs, I found that only a few first team coaches and only four managers (including assistant managers) were black ex-players. Ruud Gullit, of Chelsea Football Club, was the only black manager in the Premier League, replaced by Tigana of Fulham until his sacking. Neither was born in England. At the Professional Footballers Association, Brendon Batson was then the Deputy Chief Executive. The Football Association Council had an entirely white English membership, with only one black coach in the Football Association technical department until 2001.

Few books have explored why a small number of black ex-players were becoming coaches or were working under white managers. A notable exception to this trend was the rare recruitment and dismissal of the black management team of Ricky Hill and Chris Ramsey at Luton Football Club in the season 2000–1. The available literature on sport and racism had failed to explain how this appointment had challenged a historical trend of white men working with the same white men and moving together like a marriage throughout the different club structures in English soccer. More critically, it had failed to examine how football was developing as a cosmetic reflection of wider English society – white men in hierarchical positions, deferential black men in the support act and Asian men in administrative structures, with women restricted to the sidelines in their own segregated sport. The book was written to open up these problems, challenging a number of inherent taboos by interviewing over 200 personnel about their experiences in the institutions of coaching and management to examine how these contrasting groups saw racism operating. Table 1 shows the samples interviewed.

Table 1 Samples interviewed

Sample of black players	
Sample type	**Numbers**
Black and Asian players who failed to become coaches or managers	40
Black players who became coaches or managers	40
White male sample	
Sample type	**Numbers**
White administrators	30
White coaches	50
White managers	40

This book was also written to trace the changes made in people's approaches to racism and the unique role of their personal reflections, moving away from a view of individuals as static and the one-dimensional perceptions resulting from racism. It is a diary of a black outsider describing the interpersonal dynamics of enabling a range of people to analyse whether the opportunity to become a coach or a manager is based upon a meritocracy determined by race. Rarely do books on racism and sport reveal the tensions of the outsider, a black man revealing through the power of people's narratives and actions a system that works in contradictory ways. More crucially, the book reveals some of the ethical issues that derive from seeing racism and failing to report the discrimination that black and Asian men experience. It is a personal recording of a participant observer studying a closed part of the soccer industry, experiencing at first hand how different individuals act out their histories and privileges. Consequently it is a testimony to the silence necessary to stand back to hear, feel and thus to describe and write about racism in soccer.

Table 2 Sample of coaching courses observed

Types of course observed	Numbers
Preliminary football coaching course	15
Prep. football course	15
Full license course	5
Junior team managers' course	8
Football certificate UEFA B part one	8
Football license. UEFA B part two	2
UEFA A	2

Table 3 Sample of coaching courses participated in

Types of course participated in	Numbers
Full license	2
UEFA A conversion	1
Managers' and coaches' course	1

–1–

'House Niggers' and 'Field Niggers'
in the Culture of Playing

White Talk and the Mythologies of Race inside Sport

A number of themes have developed in 'white talk' in the genre of sports literature, most prominently the 'pathologization' of the black sportsman via an obsession with the black male body. Kane's (1971) work asserts that, by surviving
slavery, African men became more relaxed and physically stronger and thus suited
to performance on the field of play. Such ideas legitimate a 'racial biology' that
separates the black mind and the black body. The work of other white writers such
as Flemming (1995) reveals the stereotypes of the Asian athlete as small, weaker,
but more suited to intellectual pursuits, or specific sports such as cricket. These
approaches to race and sport separate black and Asian sportsmen into racial categories, polarizing the distinction between the two groups. Entine (2000) continually classifies the black body in relation to specific sports and views black men as
superior athletes simply because of their statistical success in a number of sports
during the previous four Olympic games: track, long jump and the marathon.
Entine (2000) dangerously makes the black sportsman a special obsession, whose
identity is continually rooted in different and peculiar ways to his body, on and off
the sports field, both intellectually and culturally.

Such perceptions of black sportsmen have largely resulted in damaging pathological and stereotypical images that have affected their lives outside the sports
context. Cashmore (1982) presents a negative ideal type of black family life in
which black families in Britain are unsupportive, leading to black children being
culturally disadvantaged; the school and sport systems then compensate for the
limitations of black family life:

> It is tempting to see the source of black kids' sporting involvement and success as the
> family. A rough-hewn psychological explanation would hold that, because second gen-
> eration Caribbean's and Africans in the UK are raised in single-parent families, in
> almost every case the parent being the mother, the children pass into an emotional void
> at the ages of 13 or 14 and seek out father figures in the shape of sports coaches with
> whom they form compensatory attachments. (Cashmore 1982: 79)

Cashmore portrays the black family as hard working, lacking a positive male identity and neglecting the psychological needs of young black children in the context of English society. He then projects a 'deviant' cultural pathology, which enables him to diagnose sport as a central life interest, where black men find a meaningful identity. These distinct racial attributes are discussed further in Carrington (1986), who follows a similar deficit model of black family life to that of Cashmore (1982). His comparative study of black and white pupils in sport led him to conclude that, for black children, sporting achievement compensates for academic failure, who colonize sport as an 'ethnic territory'. Victor (1993) further colludes with this impact of history by situating slavery as an ideology that instilled a selective form of breeding. This contributed towards the emergence of the black British players in the 1980s, a misconstruction that has led to this group being the central focus of this book, which explores why their lives in and outside of the sports context have been misrepresented.

The uniqueness of Davidson's (1996) work lies in her ability to describe the resilience of the black family in surviving the institutional impact of the slave period, disrupting and dislocating it in the transition from the Caribbean to British society. Davidson (1996) reveals how biological notions of race have important child-protection implications for the abuse of black people inside sport. Unfortunately this propensity to adopt a biological approach to racism and sport has led to the placement of black players into specific positions on the sports field because of their racial attributes, particularly in American football, where they had been excluded from the central back position because they are said to lack intelligence. This practice of placing black players in limited intellectual positions has been noted by Merrill and Melnick (1988) and McGuire (1991) in the playing positions of English soccer, where they found a high percentage of black players placed on the wing or in centre-forward positions. They suggest that white coaches see the black body as only operating through natural speed and physical strength and unable to be trusted to make decisions in vital positions in midfield.

This continual link between race, biology and competence in relation to the black sportsman should be seen in the context of the ways in which white men develop patterns of actions that reinforce the ideology that black men do not have sufficient intelligence. In the British context of soccer, Vasili (1998) challenges these historical myths through his biography of Arthur Wharton, the first black player in English soccer, broadening the study of racism within a class analysis. He looks historically at the emergence of black players and approaches racism by examining how black players were identified as different within the locations of English soccer because of their skin colour:

> If black players are assessed as black players first and players second this creates for them a social context which sets them apart from their white colleagues. To ignore this

and assess them only as footballers is both insensitive and selective. Their colour is an integral part of their experience. (Vasili 1998: 7)

Vasili (2000) analyses the barriers faced firstly by African men – from the arrival of Caribbean players to the actual emergence of the black British players in the period 1890–1960 – without fully developing how whiteness and class created the types of exclusionary cultures they were moving into. This failure to examine how whiteness emerges in the English game is partially addressed in the work of Carrington and McDonald (2001) who break the traditions of seeing biological and cultural forms of race as fixed. They look at sport as a zone of multicultural and nationalistic identities. Sport thus becomes a space of social contestation and cultural differences, as referenced in the work of Back, Crabble and Solomos (2001), who examine the changing spheres and forms of racism in soccer by analysing the important relationships between race, society and soccer. Unfortunately the literature in relation to black men in sport is still restricted to white biographers' preoccupation with seeing them as strange, signalling a disquieting newness in English soccer. For instance Woolnough's (1983) notion of 'black magic' symbolized black British players as having special mythical qualities, which set them aside from their white working-class colleagues during the 1980s. He suggests that they operate through a natural instinct and unstructured patterns of skills that make them impossible to coach.

This need for black players to assimilate through sport enabled Glanvill (1996) to talk about a player like Ian Wright as a problematic young black man from a dysfunctional childhood, who is normalized by obtaining citizenship within the white working-class masculine codes of soccer. Unfortunately Glanvill in a later *Daily Mail* article repeats the stereotype of the uneducated and uncivilized black child who acts out his rebellion in a current sports culture of black players with too much money and not enough sense. This theme, which sees sport as civilizing the new black British soccer player, is articulated in Hill's (1982) analysis of John Barnes by placing the issues of race within a cultural and political context. He uses Barnes' experiences to explore the pressures black players confront in an industry that shapes their identity by demanding that they 'play the white man' on white men's terms. Unfortunately the autobiographical text of white players and managers pays little attention to these terms in their relationships with black players. When they do speak about race it is often couched in crude racist ways. Atkinson's (1998) reference to the change in attitude in the second generation of black players, who think that 'life owes them a living'; and 2004 reference to 'lazy niggers'. Clough's (1994) perception of Justin Fashanu as a difficult, confused, 'black poof' shows that black players are only accepted when subservient or when they do not break the homophobic codes that hold men together across the colour line. What comes through in the autobiographies of 'football men' like Graham (1996), Charlton (1995) and

Dalglish (1996) is that they don't have to think about issues of racism. The routines that define the nature of the game's professional culture are not something of which they are conscious; they simply don't have to acknowledge the privileges of being white men and, as a result, the issue of race is simply deemed irrelevant. The failure of white men to recognize their actions as leading to institutional forms of exclusion in the structures of football is best illustrated by Kelly's (1999) reluctance, as the chief executive, to disclose how processes of racism and inequality take place in the governing body, the Football Association.

Unfortunately the autobiographical texts of black players have not offered sufficient evidence regarding the hidden ideological, political and cultural forms of racism that operate inside soccer. Gullit's (1997) refusal to name himself as black, adopting the identity of the 'overseas coach', reveals the pressures placed on black men to disguise their experiences of racism in the game. Whilst Ferdinand (1997) and Cole (1999) make more concrete links between racism through the images of black players as having 'a chip on their shoulder', these acts are described as isolated moments. Barnes (1999), however, links the pathologizing of the black soccer player to wider processes in society by describing a change from the overt racist culture of white football crowds, to a more covert form of whiteness in management, which continually selects white coaches and managers. Earle (1998) similarly sees soccer as reflecting external forms of structural racism, openly acknowledging a lack of willingness from within the white institutions of soccer to trust black men with the responsibility of being coaches and managers. The recent explosion of books from black players has consisted simply of diary reflections of their experiences of playing, a trend that does not really go into any details to describe the changing faces of forms of racism. Unfortunately the absence of an Asian player's autobiographical reflection, with only Bains and Patel (1996) offering a biography of Rick Heppolate, Chris Dolby and Jimmy Khan, means the most long-term indication of how racism operates in sport and society can be read most consistently through the black British experience.

When issues of race identity and exclusion have been explored in the context of English soccer, the literature has been primarily concerned with problems of fan behaviour and the connection between racism and 'football hooliganism' (Taylor 1982; Williams, Dunning and Murphy 1984; Williams 1991; Williams 1994). Unfortunately the pattern has been to assess racism as only having one marker, which can be seen in the behaviour of white men on the field or in the stadium. This failure to explore how white men perpetuate racism takes places by a fixation with the black athlete as pathological, thus making their own culture normal and taken for granted. In the context of sport in general, Hoberman (1997) suggests that the 'athleticizing of the black mind' leads the black sportsman to internalize his position on the field, as a commodity, with a high price. But unfortunately again Hoberman (1997) focuses on the ideological effects of race stereotyping without revealing how the actions of white men create the stereotypes experienced by black sports men, which they may internalize. This is because 'race' is never seen as patterns of social action through which whiteness emerges as an identity. So in this sense 'race' is not a biological fact, it must be seen as a socially constructed and politically constituted phenomenon. This means we can move beyond generalizing the experiences of black players, as demonstrated in Szymanski's (1993) work on the inequality of the payment structure of professional footballers. Szymanski (1993) found less money was paid to black players than to their white counterparts, despite a higher level of performance. Shropshire's (1996) study showed how black athletes preferred to have white agents because they believed they could negotiate better deals. In both these studies the power of whiteness to instil inferiority and dependency in the black athlete in relation to white men as conscious or unconscious is never explored.

This reluctance to understand why the black sportsman is continually misconstructed has evolved because of the lack of a coherent approach to explain the relationships between their experiences of racism in and outside of sport. Ashe (1993) attempted to analyse this relationship through the experiences of popular sporting icons of the last hundred years in other sports. He focuses particularly on the black boxers Jack Johnson and Muhammad Ali, to illustrate the way that American sport mirrors wider racial and political forms of exclusion. The implication in the context of America sport is that black men have very limited control in an industry where they are defined simply as physical objects. One of the reasons why the experiences of black soccer players also become generalized in soccer is because of the crude way racism and inequality have been explained through a very broad hegemonic model of sport and society. Hargreaves (1986) sees sport as a cultural and political form that determines working-class formations within a bourgeois hegemonic model, from the nineteenth century to the period of post-modern Britain. Race is then marginalized within these class relationships and thus racism is seen to operate through racial stereotypes or acts of xenophobia rather than the way white men pathologize the black sportsman.

Black Writers Strike Back

To really understand the pathologization of black players it is important to link their experiences more clearly to the ideological factors of racism that operate outside the institutions of soccer. In terms of the relationship between ideologies of race, society and sport, James (1967) as a black theorist more specifically captures how race is positioned within a hegemonic class society from slavery, to the 'Victorian era' and on to the early 1950s. The strength of James (1967) is that he examines the relationship between perceptions of skin colour, class, nationalism and professional competence inside sport. James (1967) describes how dark-skinned cricket players from the Caribbean were excluded from the position of captaincy, which was given to white English men: 'Yes they are fine players but funny isn't it they cannot be responsible for themselves, they will always need a white man to lead them' (James 1967: 232). This comment has important implications for the perceptions made of black men in English soccer. James' (1967) analysis of cricket illustrates how institutional cultures within sport mirror and enact processes of white supremacy. This power of whiteness is described in the work of Welsing (1991) in which whiteness has 'symbolic' implications for representations, images and roles that are fixed and dominated by white men. Similarly and more powerfully hooks (1991) describes the important psychological impact whiteness imposes upon the other and for excluded communities who fail to enjoy the privileges that come with being white. This analysis can be linked to the power of white men to use skin colour as an indicator of competence to explore how racism operates in the relationship between sport and society when considering the emergence of black players in the 1980s. I suggest Gilroy's (1987) work on how black is missing from the Union Jack is pertinent to examining the judgement made about whether it was possible to be both black and English when finding a place in the institutions of English sport. More specifically, it is through the relationships between men as coaches, managers and spectators that these tensions between race and nationality, between blackness and Englishness, between competence and fitting in, are revealed. Gilroy's (1993) idea of double consciousness adopted from the work of Du Bois (1903), particularly the notion of hybridity becomes useful in exploring how black men at this time make sense of their identity in moving from Africa and the Caribbean to the context of English society. These complex transitions lead to levels of consciousness in the different ways they adjust to the cultures of English football and this depends upon Rodney's (1982) theory of the colonial balance sheet of imperialism. This theory helps to assess how post-colonialism has taken away the cultural and racial identity of the outsider, and put pressures on them to assimilate. This price of race assimilation can be understood through Fanon's work (1967) that sees black men developing their place in the social world through their relationships with white men. This can be explored in the context of sport when black men relate to white men as potential employers. Black players, particularly in the 1980s, had to make a number of cultural changes to fit into English soccer and to contest the stereotype of the division between their body and their mind.

The Significance of Black Players in English Soccer

I remember speaking to two lads at that time, you were talking about the late 1970s and the early 1980s and racial abuse was at its height. I remember going out at West Ham, picking up a banana and throwing it to Cyrille, it use to be the instant reaction to that kind of abuse. There was a lot of grounds that you went to and there would be the National Front out side They said we don't need all this, a lot of black players said we don't need this aggravation. (Brendon Batson)

Brendon's comment illustrates the pernicious form of racism black players experienced in their emergence in the 1980s, the explicit forms confronted in relation to white crowds. The historical and contemporary influences of these processes were dependent upon the different cultural journeys made by black players, generally into London and Midland clubs, because of the patterns of migration from the Caribbean and Africa. They mainly played for clubs in London and in the Midlands. Hamilton (1982), focuses on the prominent black players of this period: Clyde Best, Ady Coker, Luther Blissett, Bob Hazel, Cyrille Regis, Laurie Cunningham, Garth Crooks, Viv Anderson, Vince Hillarie, Paul Davis, Chris Houghton and George Berry. He gives little consideration to other factors that affected their lives in the transition into England, especially the role of their families.

The tendency has thus been to look at the period from the 1970s to the 1990s as a time in which black players simply increased in numbers in both the Football League and the newly constituted Premier League of 1992. According to Vasili (1998) black players represented 4 per cent of the playing staff in the 1970s, increasing to 25 per cent in the 1980s and declining to 15 per cent at the present time. At present there is no South Asian player in the professional game. So it is important to focus on the routes and conditions by which black players entered the game and which influenced the types of racism they encountered. Most black players would have played for a school or a non-league team, being scouted and offered a trial resulting in an offer of apprenticeship, in contrast with the academy structure of today, which takes players from the age of nine. The cultural pressures of being inside English soccer can only be detected by analysing how black players rationalized their early experiences. For example in an interview with Colin Parker in his home in Leeds, he talked about his life as a child coming into the English game. He was born in St Kitts and came to England at the age of nine from a close knit family. He was in one of the few black families who lived in the area at the time, as he talked of a sense of being overwhelmed as the only black player during a trial at Wolverhampton Football Club: 'At Wolves a scout asked me to go for a trial and I was the only black kid and it was the first time I felt discriminated against and I was the only kid that didn't get a kick of the ball' (Colin Parker). For Colin, the isolation of being the only 'black child' is articulated by not getting a kick of the ball as his first subjective experience of being excluded. This produced a link between these two social worlds, of being different in the world of soccer because of his skin colour, which was reinforced by the fact that he belonged to one of the few black families in the area. Colin sees that this experience of being different may be based on being introduced to a system in which he's made to feel an outsider because he is physically different. If we compare how Colin rationalizes his experiences of being introduced to a soccer culture as a black person with the experiences of Brendon Batson we see that coming into the English game is not always the same:

> I didn't put a great deal on it, as many players would tell you of that era coming through the youth team we were usually the only black players, there were no other black players at Arsenal and I was the only black player at Cambridge. Other people put more on the fact we were black players than black players themselves. (Brendon Batson)

Brendon came from St Lucia to England at the age of ten; he seems to accept being the only black player as a normal part of being in English football. Although he may not look like a white man, he can still be accepted by reducing the importance of his skin colour.

These two responses show that the experiences of being stereotyped as different are determined by the subjectivity of the black player in adapting to English soccer. We can thus disprove the current belief that black players are all the same and that they experience being seen as different in the same way.

These processes of consciousness in relation to the importance of one's skin colour were shaped by the second generation of black families born outside England who influenced how black players confronted the barriers to their acceptance. Their acceptance will partially be determined by how they internalize with their parents' experiences of racism in English society in a range of different institutions. This is captured in the following interview with a black player, in his sports office, illustrating the fears black families had for their sons in English football. Frank was born in south London whereas both parents were born in Jamaica. He talked about the difficulties facing his family, the lack of jobs and the way his mother feared for his safety in going into a profession where there were very few black people:

> My parents didn't want me to go into soccer because they felt that black players weren't treated right at that time. My mother had to do the mothering and the fathering, and she might have to pick up the pieces, there wasn't a father around. (Frank Lee)

This comment illustrates a fear among black families that their sons would be abused in football stadiums – a fear made more real in this example by the absence of a father figure to protect this black player. The temptation here is to follow the trend of pathologizing the black family (Cashmore 1982), which potentially invalidates the experiences of racism in English soccer. But more crucially for the early black families, football was not sold as a viable career; it was formed in a completely different tradition, as revealed in this next quotation:

My dad always big up on having a trade, my brother said you have got to have a trade. All I wanted to do was to play football, but they didn't take it seriously, because there weren't a lot of black players playing football. And my older brother looked at me and said why you want to play football for that's a white man's game. (Darren Smith)

Darren's parents were born in Jamaica and he was one a few black players who made it into the professional game at this time. Consequently the lack of insight into football as an industry with proper jobs leads to a dilemma and a conflict between the cultural demands of his family regarding a career and a new culture inside football. The central theme that resonates from this comment is football as a place where black players were entering, viewing it as white, an assumed naturalized masculine space for white men. It is important to look at the features of whiteness that create this reaction in black families in relation to their sons entering such a profession when they had no experience of the codes and customs of white men. One of the major reasons for the low regard given to a career in soccer by black families may be related to it being a territory in which subliminally the concept of the black male body has travelled from the period of slavery when it was again valued primarily for its physical prowess. As Kovel (1988) shows, a psychology of racism categorized black men through their bodies during the period of slavery. He describes a dominant form of racism that existed during slavery with large numbers of black slaves situated in the American south who were in direct contact with an open, expressive type of physical and verbal abuse. The black male body was brutalized through the rituals of hanging and lynching and, as Kovel (1988) illustrates, the black male body became objectified as a property:

> The American slave owner went one step further in cultural development: he first reduced the human side of the black slave to a body and reduced the body to a thing: he dehumanised the slave, made him quantifiable and therefore absorbed him into a rising world of markets of productive exchange. (Kovel, 1988: 18)

The ideological connection I want to consider here between these two periods is the way the black male body is similarly catergorized in soccer, which may contribute towards the fears black families may have of similar forms of abuse. It is important to mention the huge psychological affect slavery had on the black family. As Davidson (1996) explores, it violated the family through violent abusive moments, the moments of rape and of separation, and most significantly it stamped and owned the black body. The English game during the 1980s was a location where a similar objectification of the black male body took place, in a sports culture that limited black players' identity to their body. This comment from David Boyce captures the experiences of black players trying to challenge these race stereotypes attached to their bodies:

I think there was a perception that we couldn't think, we couldn't read the game, but surely we have turned that around, with players like Paul Rose and Darren Smith. They can now see it's not just about speed, skill and strength. When I first started playing the cliché was that they were not disciplined, and all they wanted to do was run and go out dancing and to go to a night-club and anytime they told you anything they put it down to having a 'chip on your shoulder'. (David Boyce)

This comment suggests that black players during the 1980s knew that these mis-representations of their lives are taking place, and ironically once they attempted to break these stereotypes of speed and strength they became vulnerable to another set of catorgorizations in relation to their resistance to these terms.

The Echoes of Slavery on the Playing Field

The football field in the 1980s contained a specific echo of slavery – an historical period in which black men were valued for their bodies and placed in the planta-tion field. In the plantation field they were controlled and abused by their white slave masters, ordered into specific labour demands, murdered when failing to comply, and only a few black men were allowed to work in the slave master's house, receiving better treatment. Malcolm X (1965) made a number of complex divisions between these black men, ranging from skin colour to the distinction between a category of black men who worked in the field, which he referred to as the 'field nigger', and those who worked in the house, which he called the 'house nigger'. The 'field niggers' were more resistant to racism because they experienced the more violent acts of white men, whereas the 'house niggers', who received better treatment, were more compliant towards white men. Malcolm X (1965) explores the different locations and the different acts of repression and controls during slavery:

Since slavery, the American white man has always kept some handicapped Negroes, who fared much better than the black masses suffering and slaving in the fields. The white man has these 'house' and 'field' Negroes for his special servants. He threw them crumbs from his own table; he even let them eat at his table. (Malcolm X, 1967: 340)

The plantation field may appear a radical metaphor, but it has similarities within the football field because of the similar processes of racism in relation to how black men were treated by white men in relation to their bodies. The similarity res-onates here in being under the control of white men who use their powers in dif-ferent ways, the whip being replaced by the abusive word, and lastly the manner is which the school and soccer replaces the absent black father figure. The transfer of the black male from one institution, the school, to another, the playing field, has very important implications in relation to the ways he is seen and treated by white men. A black player who made his debut in the 1980s talks about being frightened and unaware of the level of abuse he would suffer in the playing field:

> I was playing one of my first games for Man City at Derby I remember going over to take a corner and I was pelted by bananas, they were falling on to the pitch besides me and I was young probably 23 or 24 and I thought 'shit, what is this', what have I let myself in for. (David Boyce)

David's position on the pitch by the corner flag just about to take a corner, close to the crowd and being pelted by bananas, reflects the legacy and actions of white men from the period of slavery: a legacy that sees black players as less than human and thus deserving to be treated like animals. The banana represents a symbol of power to dehumanize, a form of racism by which white men portray black people as savages. The shock and disorientation in this player helps him cope with these acts of white men as his first survival tactic. His reluctance to be openly defiant should not be seen as submissive or similar to how the 'house nigger' in the period of slavery accepted these acts of white men and was accepted into their homes. This represents a series of sophisticated strategies to be safe, to perform and disconnect his anger and disgust for the period of ninety minutes where he cannot change these historical patterns of white male behaviour. These approaches can both invert and normalize these symbols of white racism as part of being a professional footballer in English soccer. He learns that although he is vulnerable to these violent acts by white men, he has to conceal, politically, how he feels in his internal world to guarantee a place amongst his white team mates and managers. Although black players may experience similar acts of racism to those experienced by the 'field nigger' in the plantation field during the period of slavery, their responses are far more multifaceted. The echo of the plantation field within the football field is personified further in this story from Tony Francis:

> I suppose it was at Leeds, not playing for Leeds but playing at Leeds for Portsmouth where you had people shouting for ninety minutes 'shoot that nigger', 'kill that nigger'. I had that at Leeds, I had it for a spell at Portsmouth, and my own fans had a go at me for a couple of games. A minority of them because I was the only black man to play down there for a long time. I had an experience at Crystal Palace where a fan came on and abused me physically, smacked me and I had to leg it. (Tony Francis)

In this comment, Tony talks about the abuse he experienced from white supporters. The terms 'shoot that nigger', 'kill that nigger' and the act of being attacked by a white man reflect the way in which black men in soccer during this period were subjected to similar assaults to those that took place on the plantation field. The drama, being pelted with a banana, the race narrative, the word 'nigger', being physically threatened resonated throughout the accounts of the black players

I interviewed. They represent the visible forms of racial abuse that become an integral part of being a 'black' professional soccer player. They also reflect the processes of racism, institutional to the role of being in a professional football culture in which a public deference towards the racism of white men is never openly challenged:

> At the time you had your silly racist jokes but the crowd especially up north at Sunderland was nasty and one of the things I was told to expect was a lot of chants and name calling. But if you went further on in your career you had to put things like this outside of your system and go out there and prove you're the best player on the park and smile and that would put you in the right frame of mind. So things like that were explained to me very early on in my career. (Frank Lee)

It appears that black players have to deal with two realities: firstly having to accept, as a routine, racial abuse from white fans; secondly, in their contact with white coaches and managers (the apparent white slave masters because of their power), they are forced always to be compliant with these acts as part of the performance of being in the English game. Consequently Frank Lee illustrates two contrasting but interrelated forms of white male behaviour: the onside racism from football crowds, shaped by the offside unconscious form of racism from his white manager by the way he is instructed to accept abuse as part of being in football. Frank becomes so embroiled in 'playing the white man' through this role given to him by his white manager, which is similar to the roles white slave masters enforced on black slaves, that racism becomes legitimate and registered as a justified routine for a black professional soccer player. This connection between legitimacy and performance means black players are continually involved in an unfolding complex drama that links to the cultural sacrifices needed to co-exist inside soccer. Racism can then change its form from the pitch, where it is more open, to being more difficult to identify and name when enacted by white professionals behind the scenes as revealed in this next comment:

> Things weren't easy and society accepted black players as casual in the field of play. When I got my contract I felt part of the family. I had been classed as an equal under the same badge as a family. That's as close as it gets, as if you're in it together from Monday to Saturday. I was a pretty easy person to get on with, pretty polite and as a black person you had to be double polite to be accepted you had to keep people happy. (Frank Lee)

Frank Lee begins to unpack some of the social pressures that were placed on black players to adjust and integrate in English football clubs in the 1980s and 1990s. He describes the silent and powerful pressure to be the subservient black man in an attempt to appease white men. He reveals the psychological pressures imposed in order to obtain a contract, to become part of, but not necessarily inte-grated into the white 'football family'. This leads to black players in this period reconciling themselves with the demands of white coaches and managers, as a central issue of complicity:

> So long as you could toe the line, you got your racist jokes like my coach use to call me 'cherry blossom' not knowing it was a racist joke and the other players could pick up on that. You would get the trends where people have seen something on television and they would try it out on you. (Colin Parker)

Colin raises the problems faced when hearing racist comments of which white men are oblivious. The term 'cherry blossom' refers to a dark colour shoe polish that was used negatively and placed him in a position of acknowledging its racist content, but he had to 'toe the line' without defiance as an exchange for being accepted. His approach to the stereotype is filtered through a veil that analyses the range of actions possible for him in front of white men. Even when he performs as white men require, there is no certainty of acceptance, so that playing into this culture of English soccer is a gamble. It means tolerating degradation by white men in a system where he cannot change on his own.

More generally black players do not always know the implications of being inte-grated:

> With Mike Henry it was like a Territorial Army. He was big on discipline; it was not a great deal of how are you. A similar type of personality to Alan Mark. Very, very hard, a little bit of an eccentric, very, very disciplined. He was the hardest one to get on with. I preferred Gerry Webster. he was soft and a father figure. All I tried to do was to keep the manager happy. (Frank Lee)

This comment reveals the complexity of confronting the different ways white men maintain their privileges by assuming that black players respond voluntarily and on their terms. Their approach, whether based on authority or softness, repre-sents a power naturalized within the settings of football that leads to confusion over black players' civil rights. Black players continually face these judgments over their integration in locations of football. Such judgements operate on a more implicit level in relationships with white coaches. This is best reflected in an inci-dent in Ian Wright's autobiography (1997), in which race may or may not be a factor:

> Bruce Rioch also pulled me aside one day and told me he found my language unac-ceptable. Psychology plays a huge part in football and relationships between managers and players, even though I was partly to blame with my attitude. I think that Bruce Rioch made a big mistake psychologically. I can take somebody tearing into me if I've

done something wrong, but the big stick does not always work. The managers who have got the best out of me know that I need an arm around my shoulder, sometimes a quiet word of encouragement every now and then. (Ian Wright 1997: 21)

It is important to contextualize this interaction as one taking place between a high-profile black forward and a white manager who has just arrived at the football club, who is seen as having a controlling approach, which the black player rebels against. This perception of the need to be treated with the 'big stick', to be talked to in the 'right language', may seem to replay one of the historical relationships between the white adult and the black child, the one who has authority and the one who needs to be controlled. It has a historical connotation in the context of football, and other institutions, particularly education, in that the power is always with the white authority figure. Football in this context, with more black players, becomes a stage where these subliminal processes and covert relationships are acted out. In this specific case the black player internalizes what is permissible from the white male authority figure – to 'tear into me' or, in contrast, putting an 'arm around my shoulder' or having a 'quiet word'. These are the range of options for interpreting the situation open to him in buying into the professional cultures of football as a black player, although the situation may simply be seen as a personality clash that all players go through. The significance here is that for black players their managers or their coaches will always be white; they don't have the luxury of not having to see race as redundant; they don't have the power to simply analyse these problems without some reference to how racism may operate as a factor. These are processes and power dynamics that do not always avail themselves to open scrutiny, as black players are struggling for the same kinds of freedoms as white men, to be accepted as individuals. In football settings, however, these freedoms are influenced by how black players reconcile themselves to the pressures, acting out acceptance on terms they may find reprehensible.

Although the English game, especially the Premier League, has seen a reduction in racial abuse towards black players' in the twenty-first century, on the international level there are still question marks about black players' status and citizenship as English players that do not face their white male counterparts. The emergence of black players in the white shirt of the national team and their acceptance as being both English and being black, in and outside of the game, is shaped by white men.

I want to pick just one important moment that reveals the challenge for black players in obtaining a passport as fully English, stamped by white crowds at the international level, as distinct from the test of regional attachments at club level:

One game particularly when we played away and we were warming up and somebody shouted to Paul Harrison remember where you come from you were once a West Ham player and now you're just a black bastard. But you know deep down in your mind, I am not saying everybody who supports England, if they could have an all white team then they would have it. That's the feeling you get from different sectors of football. (Tom Stevens)

In this interview with Tom he describes vividly how difficult it is to be permitted to travel uninhibited into the national pride of white men in the international stadium. Tom points to a form of racism in English soccer that questions black player's legitimacy within the white imagination. He can play for England, whilst he can be seen as different because he is not white. This is similar to the first experiences of black players in the early 1970s. These crude moments of racism are captured in the display of the St George flag, the sentiment of the song *Rule Britannia* ('Britons never, never, never, shall be slaves') sung by white people and by a growing number of black spectators in the stadiums, ensure that black players face the test of whether they can be fully English while they have a different colour skin. Despite the cultural changes made by black players to demonstrate their Englishness – in going out with white women and embroiling themselves in the professional culture of soccer – their acceptance is determined by criteria they have no control over. Black players can perform acts of nationalism, but their multicultural approach to Englishness may not receive the social approval of white men, especially outside the context of the industry, even when white men display support for them as other countries abuse black players now playing for England.

The theme of how the acts of white men impact on the performances of black players inside the English context of English football can be examined more critically by looking at black players' experiences with other white players on a field of play that links to a wider culture that excludes them.

Racism and the Interface with White Players

The relationships between black men and white men on the field of play reveals a complicated and contradictory form of racism captured in this interview with Tony Davis, one of the first black players to play for Manchester United. During our telephone conversation he reflected on the ways that he was treated by white players and laughed very loudly:

> You've got players saying 'you black bastard' and 'I will break your legs'. It went on right throughout my career. The irony of it is that you get this and they want to apologise afterwards. You would see them in the bar afterwards and they would say 'sorry about calling you a black bastard'. It wasn't racism it was like the enemy, what can we do to weaken them? (Tony Davis)

Tony articulates the ambiguous nature of racist language. Coded in the playing field it represents a form of sportsmanship, it is meant to 'put him off his game'.

In the bar after the game, the apology reclassifies the racist comment; it becomes a harmless gesture, which makes black players vulnerable to the accusation of being 'oversensitive' or 'temperamental'. Black players then find it difficult to hold white men accountable when racist comments are translated as 'industrial language'. It is seen as a legitimate form of competition between men. How black players deal with racist remarks will depend upon how they are actually perceived, which depends on the situation and how they link these experiences as being both inside English society and inside the English game:

> As a black footballer you are easily accepted. There are black people out there struggling for a lot less and I know the struggles. As a black footballer you are more easily accepted, so people see the colour and they say its OK they are a footballer. You have to be a strong character to stand up to things if you're the only black player, especially if they say they don't mean it. It's easier if you have the backing of the black community. If you're the only one you're not sure if the other black players will come with you. (Ian Harris)

Consequently racism can change in form from the pitch, where it is more open and audible, to being more difficult to identify and name when enacted by white professionals behind the closed doors where it is invisible to the wider public.

The 'Chip on the Shoulder' and the Hidden Nature of Racism

The power of white coaches and managers to shape black players' acceptance can be illustrated more explicitly through the notion of the 'chip on the shoulder', a phrase that has become a test of black players' ability to adapt to the cultures of English football. The idea of the 'chip on the shoulder' has often been used to describe people who have problems with authority, who are rebellious and use excuses for their failure. It was often used in relation to black players who came into the English game during the 1980s as revealed by this black player:

> If you speak to white coaches they don't know how to speak to a black child or a black player. They would say they have a 'chip on their shoulder'. When I first started at QPR, there were a couple of black lads and I would often hear the Youth Development officer say, I don't know why they have got a 'chip on the shoulder'. We did have this white goalkeeper, who had this same attitude as this black fellow. I use to say why hasn't he got a 'chip on his shoulder'? And they use to say he's all-right he just takes it hard. So why does he take it hard, and why has he got a 'chip on his shoulder'. (Les Frank)

More crucially the 'chip on the shoulder' has broader social implications that filter into football in the ways white men can affix attitudes to race. It exempts white men from the same criticism. They can express their anger, which is seen as a quality white men demonstrate to succeed. The notion of the 'chip on the shoulder' is continually applied to black players by white coaches creating an inherent and ongoing question mark about their ability to succeed. These judgements impose inflexible notions of black players who are only allowed to behave in relation to the demands of white coaches and managers. This is expressed in the following interview with a black player, born in south London, who played during the late 1980s:

> Harry Best took over. At the time I had dreadlocks and was called into the office. I was asked why I had dreadlocks and I said that it was an affirmation of my African heritage. They said it wasn't appropriate. Harry Best told me to cut them off. I told him apart from the fact that I was 26 or 27 years of age and nobody had told me how to cut my hair it would offend my whole heritage. And if I was to get my hair cut he should do some elocution lesson to get rid of his Scottish accent. (Ian Smith)

Ian's challenge to this white Scottish coach makes visible a form of racism that challenges the heritage and political and cultural positioning of black players in English soccer. His hairstyle tested the codes expected of professional players. If Ian was compliant with what his white coach wanted him to look like, he would conform to the ethos of the football culture in which he cannot flag up this disrespect for his heritage, so the whistle of racism would never be blown on or off the playing field. Ian's situation was not simply a call for an appreciation of his African heritage, but an assertion of his difference that exposed the limitations of his manager as a white man in failing to accept black players and all the different customs and perceptions of the past they bring from outside of the context of the English game into the setting of the pitch and the training ground. This difference based on race is further highlighted in Ian's comments about another incident on the training pitch:

> I was down at Torquay and they had an assistant manager there by the name of Terry Walsh. I had been down there a couple of days and it got down to a five a side and he said 'we have the white team over there and the "coons" and "niggers" over there'. I said you do know what my name is, if you can't use my name then don't speak to me at all, but don't call me 'nigger' or a 'coon'. I said, 'if you're going to refer to me in those derogatory terms I will tear you head off. (Ian Smith)

Ian highlights the crude racist caricatures that reflect white men's ability from the stadium to the training ground, to dehumanize black players who seemingly should not question their authority. Ian's option is to speak out in defiance – a response that is often used by white men as part of the concept of being men. In the case of a black man like Ian, he becomes exposed again to this accusation of having a 'chip on his shoulder' when he challenges another white man. In the context of a training group Ian is relegated back to the status of being a 'nigger' no matter how unwittingly this term is being used. The act of separating him from his white colleagues on the base of race reveals the unconscious form of exclusion that starts from within the football club as mirroring the processes of racism that operate both historically and in the context of English society.

This problem of the agreements and the behaviours that are shared across the colour line was tested on a far more provocative level in the case of Justin Fashanu in relation to the boundaries of race, masculinity and sexuality. Justin was born in Nigeria, brought-up by white foster parents and celebrated as a big, strong archetypical fast forward, who personified the expensive black male commodity, a teenage one million purchase. After a promising career wavered, he sold his story to the newspaper and revealed he was gay. He eventually hanged himself after an allegation of sexual abuse on a young white male. Before his suicide his brother commented 'he did not want him around, footballers close rank' thus demonstrating the discomfort of a culture that could not accommodate black men who 'played the white man' by crossing the sexual lines that hold men together. On several levels, Justin disrupted the manner in which black players had been stereotyped in the English game. On the field of play he was bold, brave and he was a team player. Once he disclosed his sexuality, he shattered the masculine illusion of soccer and revealed a possibility that a black man in sport could exploit his body in two contradictory ways. Firstly, for fitting the stereotype of the fast forward, but secondly and more crucially, using his body to sexually abuse another white man. Justin's case makes it explicit that to be accepted, to be normalized as an English player, it was more important to act white, but also to be straight and heterosexual as part of the unwritten agreement amongst players.

Ironically Justin had damaged and severely dented the politics of black masculinity in the context of football. He raised the possibility of being aggressive on the field of play, whilst off it he could sleep with the enemy, most significantly another white man – one of a group who had been the oppressors of the black experience both inside football, and outside football in terms of excluding them from accessing and being represented in the structures of British society.

They Think it's All Over: Facing New Racism and Exclusions

One of the biggest fears for players after putting their boots up, no longer having a contract and finding that their role as professional soccer players has ended, is the fact that they cannot play for ever. They can either stay on as coaches or managers, or in another related capacity, or most commonly, they can leave the game:

> I was naïve at the time but never thought I would ever stop playing football, I thought I could play forever. I thought I had enough put aside; I just wanted a little mortgage

to say that's what I got out of it. I wanted to be a coach but I don't think the opportunities were always there. There are times when I wanted to be a coach, it's not only a matter of colour, but there are lot more white coaches than coloured ones. But I would like to think that any black player that has been in the game and has done a coaching badge would be equal to a white coach. (Frank Lee)

Frank talks about ending his career and finding out he wasn't good at anything else. He realized the importance of his skin colour in competing for jobs as a coach against his white male counterparts. He justifies his exit from the industry with the rationalization that it is a space for white players – a rationalization similar to that expressed by black parents. He internalizes the idea that to become a coach is impossible due to the greater numbers of white men in this industry. He thus revisits the structural forms of racism that Derrick Morris highlights as being similar to the types of racism experienced by black people outside of English soccer:

It is only now that an influx of black players who have packed in the game and are trying to get into management. I think it is just a matter of time will tell. If I had to predict I know a lot of black guys who have had 10–15 years in football, who may have got management and coaching qualifications, who are seeking employment in that field. What the statistics show, it will take time; it may be hard for them to get a job. Like in society black people find it hard to get employment at management level and I don't think that football will be any different. (Derrick Morris)

The illusion sold to this black player was that time rather than discrimination influences his progression and disguises the fact that in this evolutionary process white men develop exclusionary processes that black players have to face in this transition into coaching and management. Geoff Webb, as one of the most prominent black players during the period under consideration, brings to life the concerns black players confront in an industry where white men cannot connect these historical processes of power to the dynamics that exist within soccer. He very acutely links these two worlds, the world of football and the outside social world from which black players had become alienated:

There's still racism, it is as simple as that. We all try to put different labels on it, but they don't have the faith in black people, because of the bad press we get. They trusted us in the field but will they trust us to lose a few million of their money. I don't think black people are any worse than white people, we are told we are laid back and black people get labeled that way. It's plain and fucking simple there are certain people out there that don't want black people to get on, they want to keep them where they are. We've got our token black so that's ok, but that's fucking rubbish. (Geoff Webb)

Geoff's comments reveal a situation in which white players at the end of their playing career will have a better chance to participate in the football industry because of being trusted. Despite an investment in a new multiculturalism in the playing side, this ethos fails to reach all spheres of football. The preoccupation with the delayed emergence of Asian players distracts from English clubs' refusal to inspire the transition of black players into coaching and management. It distracts from the process of examining and making transparent the ways in which white-ness operates to maintain its power at this level of the football industry. A league table of race positioning is now visible: white men in charge, black players finding they have no power in the transition from the field, whilst the Asian male is still on the bench. More critically we can see how sport mirrors the types of structural racism in society, imposing a glass ceiling so that very few black people are moving into coaching and management positions. It is important to note that the phenomena discussed in this chapter concerning the racism experienced by black players and its historical connotations, more specifically the power dynamics between black and white people, are actually occurring in other institutional settings. It is the problem that black people experience throughout English society, whether it be with the police, or the legal or educational professions. The mystery behind the processes that lead to the predominance of one group has never really been opened up for explanation.

−2−

'Playing the White Man': Meritocracy, Whiteness and the Myths of Qualifications

Racism in the Coaching Field

When professional footballers retire from the English game, attaining a coaching badge is the first step towards getting a job as a coach or a manager. Since the English Football Association made it mandatory that a UEFA A coaching badge and a Pro Licence are needed to manage in English football, the qualifications have taken on a more serious consideration for players' career development. I believe this is an unrealistic and unfair way of getting jobs in the sport as it camouflages the importance of networking, which forces black players to compromise with white men who hold the power in this industry in terms of selection, when they may not actually need this qualification.

To make visible how white men dictate the settings and the access into the coaching and management qualification we may observe how Fanon's (1967) notion of the 'white mask' shows the barriers that black players confront in making the transition into a profession that is not meritocratic. I suggest that Goffman's (1956) idea of a 'front stage' helps show how a form of racism evolves by the ways white tutors act in front of black candidates, as the public face of whiteness. It brings to light the hidden rules that shape black player's inclusion, at the 'back stage', the closed doors where an offside racism is formed in the absence of black players. Consequently the more informal the setting of the qualifications, the more hidden and the more collusive acts of exclusion operate without any level of accountability. As a result black players lose the capacity to persuade white men to be more conscious of their racism and to make it visible so they can change a very exclusive culture in which qualifications simply hide the more important selection processes that take place outside this setting.

The coaching qualification thus represents a set of traditions in English soccer where black ex-players reveal new social and cultural expectations, inside new locations, procedures, and rituals. I explored this when I participated in a range of courses between 1993 and 2003. A regime is established by the Football Association (FA) and the local county associations that administer the course, which is sanctioned by the FA Instructional Committee, made up of white men co-opted from the Army, the county associations and the universities. They approve the general structure of the course through a practical coaching 'assessment sheet', used to judge the competence of the students. The 'assessment sheet' represents an interpretative mechanism and a value judgment held by white men who assume that it transcends all race, culture or class differences. The implications of this race-neutral approach in relation to the assessment process can only be analysed in its applications to the lives of black ex-players and other groups who have not taken part in the construction of the process.

The neutrality of the qualification system can be seen by the way the course is organized and the dynamics that take place within the practical work, which comprises 60 per cent of the course. The first example of how white men colonize the course is through their instructions to engage in all the pre-course work they design; watching the English 'winning formula' coaching videos and reading the accompanying set of books. The pressure to comply with white men's expectations is reinforced by the compulsion to perform in Umbro kit at the 'front stage', the pitch, and in front of the tutors, through demands made by white men at the 'back stage'. These back stages are locations unknown and closed to black players, so it is impossible to challenge the rationale of these codes of dress. It's important to make reference to the broader front stage, the course location at the National Sports Centre in Lilleshall, in the leafy countryside of Shropshire, where a regional and historical form of racism is viewed. A distinct Englishness is revealed by 100 acres of rural, rich green land, transformed into playing fields accessed through big iron gates, along stony paths. This leads to a mansion hung with portraits of famous white Englishmen. On entry to the main building one is confronted by a notice board, with a picture of the Queen and Prince Phillip: this Building was donated to the Sports Council by the South Africa Government in 1951.

The building represents a legacy of a colonialist past, an outlay of large houses positioned some distance from the playing field. The absence of black men in these houses (reminiscent of the apartheid age in which this building was given) – both among the tutors involved and in the construction of the course – leaves important spaces in terms of language and patterns of behaviour, enabling white men to reinforce their personal histories in the format of the course. The relationship between the heritage of the building and the power of white male tutors can be analysed by examing the ways predominantly middle-class ex-teachers develop routines that are coded by specific historical patterns. Over the next fourteen days there is only one afternoon off. The day begins at 8 am, with daily meals, lectures and practical sessions in the field. Black players are located into groups and subgroups led by white ex-players, and are thus immediately placed in the subordinate position. These formations of white men lead them to formalize in the structure of the course their rituals and their perceptions of impartiality:

I don't think it matters where you come from. Everybody once they come on this course has an equal chance as anybody. It does not matter what race or what sex you are, if you are a professional player or not, or if you were a teacher, everybody is judged on the same standards. (Steven Reid, course tutor)

Steven's reluctance, through this illusion of an ethos of equality, to see how the course may discriminate against those who have not been in this environment undermines the possibility that black men can question the fairness of white men. A completely different performance is now demanded of black ex-players as the identity they shared with white men as players and as men changes when competing against them for a coaching qualification. Former white players and white tutors begin to share an identity as white men, although they may come from different backgrounds. They create an easiness in being on the course without reference to naming the convenience of being white. The forms of masculinity that went across the colour line in the playing field are replaced by black men adjusting to white men as candidates or as tutors as they arrive on the course entering the canteen area where the roll call takes place. Two come in chatting to white students, one is late, as another black ex-player scans the room looking for a safe space in a sea of white faces. He is now deprived of the luxury of simply identifying himself through the club tracksuit he wears or the people he knows. He is deprived of the advantage that white men enjoy in walking into spaces that have been created by other white men before them, where a legacy of being at home is established, a home that is in complete contradiction to the experiences of black ex-players, who are hugely outnumbered on these courses.

This legacy of being at home is further instilled by the embodiment of an all white tutor group dressed in the same uniform: Umbro hats, T-shirts, tracksuits, shorts and socks. The white course coordinator reads out the tutor groups, which retire to another room to be told about how the subgroups will operate. In all four groups a paternal image of whiteness is promoted through the selection of older well-known white ex-players, giving authority to the manner in which the course tutor outlines the expectations for the next fourteen days:

It's important that all the sessions start on time, you must be out of your room, have your breakfast and be in the lecture room by 9 am and then we come into this room for a group meeting. By the fourth day when Football Association tutors have shown you all the practical demonstrations that may be given to you as a topic, you will be given your actual topic. It's important you study it, and I will be able to give some time in relation to your organization. It is vitally important that we help each other out. All right, any questions; good, see you in the morning. (Steven Reid, course coordinator)

He stands in front of the group, clip-book in hand, arms folded, with his legs firmly apart, a military pose, without eye contact, making explicit what will be expected of the course members. The non-negotiable tone that resonates in this comment instils a confidence that can be observed through the way white men sit at the front of the class and the three black students position themselves at the back of the class. The black students' false smile, the first example of a mask, is a coded response to show to white men that they can cope with the nature of the conversion needed to acquire the coaching qualification. They conceal an internal fear about how to deal with white tutors who do not recognize the difficulties faced in moving into their zones of comfort. I talked to one of the black players in his room about what it felt like to be in this group situation having got to know him over the week:

> There are definitely more black people on the course this year but I am the only one in my group. The tutor and the other coaches without even knowing it have got a way of making you feel really isolated and for younger people it could really destroy them. If there are certain politics I think it depends what professional club you are with will influence your chance in getting the badge. It's certainly true the savages like me will need more help. (Black course member)

He looked to the ceiling in despair, and with an anxious glance, he shrugged his shoulders, as if he had had enough: his comment articulates how the cultural environment creates a loneliness, a need to be both educated and civilized by the power of white men who mystify black players, leaving them unsure how to act, to integrate, to get a coaching qualification. Black players co-exist in a social void, as they see the development of white men's comfort zones, the closed doors, both within and outside the context of the coaching qualification. The unpredictable implications of being made vulnerable to having to reproduce the expectations of white men is reflected in this quotation from Utchay: 'A black man cannot be secure in his employment by mastering his duties alone. He must study the idiosyncrasies and peculiarities of the white man at the head and study and endeavor to satisfy. For his continuation in the service depends on the will of this one individual' (Utchay 1975: 437).

Utchay articulates this sense of mystery facing black ex-players arising from the inconsistency and the unpredictability of white norms, based upon a will which is difficult to see because it is so unconscious to white men. This power of the 'will' of white men is crucial to the position of black players having to constantly be dependent on how white men judge them. Black players become prisoners to this historical theme that what white men expect them to do will not always be rational and clear to them. For example when moving into the coaching field, away from their former situation as players where black men once experienced crude derogatory forms of racism, where white men shouted racist abuse, such racsim is now replaced by white men assessing whether they are competent to be given a coaching qualification. Black ex-players' ability to adjust to the changes in white men can be observed by the ways that they interact with those who use their capacity in different ways to influence black ex-players performances. Similar to Kovel's (1988) approach to aversion, black ex-players begin to experience white men disassociating themselves from them and denying them access to the spaces where their privileges are reaffirmed through the structure of the course. These powers of white men operate through this 'will' to use informal rules to evaluate black ex-players, who are deluded into believing that a qualification is important to their career development. Advocating the importance of coaching qualifications hides the power of white men to dictate a specific coaching model, the 'command style', which is symbolic of a range of controls used throughout the coaching course. This command style is enacted during each of the sessions in which the white tutor stops the game, analyses a mistake and shows the course members how to correct the mistake. It is a style that also resonates in their control over black candidates, whose lack of involvement in this presentation then questions how authentic the performance is valued if it is not carried out by a white man. These unconscious acts of white men are further displayed in their physical demeanour and the language they use:

> Stop, stand still, and let me take your place. This is what I want you to do and do you understand? Good, now let me see you do it. Great that's exactly what I want. That's good, you have done well, so have you, you could tuck in more, and what are you doing over there half asleep. (White course tutor)

The five tutors will adopt a common body position, a legacy of their past tutors, standing on the side, away from the students, stopping the game with a large shout and slowly walking on to the pitch. They thus dictate a ritualized performance in a space where black men must show that they are comfortable in reproducing both verbally and physically. The quality of the relationships between course tutor and course members, more specifically the compliance between white tutors and black men that determines the perceptions of being able to reproduce the standards of white men, is more abstract and concealed. For example, in the coaching field the head tutor is positioned sitting in a chair wearing sunglasses, monitoring the performances of the tutors and the course members. By bringing together the whole group for a question-and-answer session, he can assess the level of compliance of the students. Black players face a dilemma as to whether white men will be consistent in the ways they see and assess them as candidates, both publicly and privately, without making any reference to their capacity to act in the same ways as white men.

To enable us to analyse the unpredictability of the white norm that black players confront, we can note two incidents that illustrate the problem in being assessed by white men in the setting of the full licence (UEFA A) course.

In the first example during one of his sessions, Marlon Jenkins was being assessed on a coaching topic, 'finishing from crosses'. He set up his session, it began and the white tutor placed himself on the opposite side of the pitch, tightly holding a clipboard with the assessment criteria, the coaching bible. The crosses were poor. As Marlon struggled to get the players to cross effectively, the white tutor then dropped his folder, the first indicator that the session was going badly and the codes of the performance were not being followed successfully. Within two minutes the white tutor had told the nearly all white players in the session what he wanted, the crosses go in and like magic, the play just happens and makes sense. Marlon took over, his voice shaky, reluctant to go in and correct mistakes, as the act of this white man arrogantly intervening had left Marlon confused. Is it purely his ability to effect the change in the performance of the players, or it is due to a deference to the tutor, who is white, in a setting where he has taught and performed before? Marlon reflects on how this moment had affected him emotionally:

> I don't know what went wrong, in all my days as a professional players I never been through anything like that before, its nothing like the pro-game, although they have taught me a lot and I have learnt a few new things. This tutor giving me bad marks and treated me just like a school kid and kept on coming in during my session, it just felt really intimidating. (Marlon Jenkins)

What lies behind Marlon's comment is a mystification around how white men seem naturally comfortable in a setting that they devised, constantly performed in and where they seem at home, a historical and cultural home that is rarely disrupted. Marlon personalizes this disadvantage and almost regresses and becomes disabled to the extent that he goes back to the power differentials felt in his childhood as a response to this fear of not knowing how these white men work this system and how they are able to make him feel so inadequate in this setting. Despite his experiences of professional soccer and teaching, he sees the power of white men to adjust and perform within their own rules within the coaching qualification setting.

Marlon's confusion about how white men operate was made further complex by having a change in tutor. During his second session, the tutor who gave Marlon his poor marks had to leave the course due to a family illness. The second white tutor, who took over the marking responsibility, spent more time coming in during the coaching session on defending. This led to a surprising new outcome, as Marlon's marks had improved considerably. In the canteen I asked Marlon about this situation as he searched around the room to see if anybody was watching. The white tutors were situated together in the corner of the room on the top table. Marlon was continually casting a suspicious look over his shoulder, not knowing how much he can disclose in case his personal comments are heard, reflecting an ongoing fear of their presence:

I can't explain it; it just seemed easier and maybe it was because I knew this tutor as we both live in the same area of Islington. Its difficult to tell how these white men think, one is really miserable and gives me good marks, the other, the 'fat destroyer', gives me poor marks. The most difficult thing is getting use to the different approaches of the tutors. I don't know if it's racism or not, but I have been all over the country as a professional player and have seen different types of racism at different clubs, so I have developed a second sense to it and you kind of expect it at different levels. The worst kind of racism is not what they say; it's what they don't say in case they are accused of being racist. (Marlon Jenkins)

From this comment it can be seen that the quality and the personal dynamics of the relationships between black ex-players and white tutors makes the assessment process more complex, especially the task of how to read the unpredictable and changing norms of whiteness. Despite the outcome, whether Marlon gets a good or a bad mark, the problem is the luxury that white men have in this context to discriminate based on their subjective feelings, where this unconscious form of racism cannot be seen by black players, who know their responses may then determine their future in the game. The outcome is that black ex-players cannot be sure that what they do on the coaching field will be the only criterion by which they will be judged.

This confusion is illustrated in an interview with another black professional player who was consistently receiving poor marks on the course. He felt that other white students, less competent than him, were receiving better marks because they got on better with the white tutors. The suspicion that white men were in a better position to pass, through their ability to operate within a mutual comfort zone, was expressed by the way he reproduced how he saw white men being so natural with each other. He stood up in the middle of the bedroom, put his hat and glasses on and brilliantly imitated the head tutor, right down to his accent. He went quiet after a period of laughter and began to reflect back on his relationship with his tutor and his poor performance. He talked as if the tutor was in front of him, thus revealing how black ex-players use their own back stage spaces to decode what white tutors represent in their lives during the course:

I just thought my tutor had very real little time for me, they said they were there to help, but during this period of time you were very lucky if you got two or three minutes with them. I feel their approach is rather teacher like and they do seem to favor the teaching approach. Their approach is rather regimental; I like to have a laugh and a joke. I don't feel there are any race problems with the tutors at the moment the only politics I can see at the moment is the preferential treatment towards those who have some link with the Football Association. (Black course member)

The comment reflects a state of isolation, abandonment, a lack of trust, the image of white teachers as army instructors who alienate those they had no previous associations with and those who do not comply with their expectations. This black ex-player's response is similar to Basso's (1979) analysis of how the Apache Indians portrayed and parodied white men who acted disrespectfully towards them: he finds a way of making sense of them outside of their space in order to cope with their cold and unpredictable ways that he sees them as intervening into his life. Thus, the way that white men are experienced raises a number of conflicts for black players in terms of how they should prepare and apply themselves to seek their acceptance. Throughout their relationships with white male tutors they face the need to perform, in an unsafe atmosphere where white men advocate equality and then can act in highly preferential ways. For example, whilst on the course a black ex-player talked about a situation when the course tutor reprimanded him for wearing a baseball cap and sun glasses and asked him not to swear in front of the players. He then put his cap on and rehearsed what the tutor had said to him and how it made him feel about this white man:

> You know that fat bastard, how dare he come over to me and tell me to take my cap off, because it didn't look appropriate for a coach. They want to get into the real world, when I'm down at my club there are no problems with me wearing a baseball cap. The funny thing about it [he begins to laugh] his fucking boss sitting in the corner with a fucking Umbro baseball cap and dark classes. Who the fuck does he think he is, not even my Father talks to me like that. And you can't swear, fucking hell does he think I am a nun or something, the fucking prick. (Black course member)

My point from this comment is that, in this paternal world of whiteness, black players feel they are being unjustly 'put into their place' by the rules made in their absence and by the way they are set by staff who decide how to apply to them. There is a powerful feeling of being destroyed and being placed in an environment in which these forms of control operate. Consequently, white men in the role of tutors can break the rules by wearing the acceptable brand of baseball cap and sunglasses, whilst the black player is told off for what is perceived as unconventional attire. Consequently the challenges to copy or parody the white man, his language, dress and actions, create an irony, with the white coach in the background wearing items of clothing associated with black culture.

This raises the problems of race as a social construction as discussed in the work of Fishkin (1993) when she talks about how much blackness enters whiteness and whiteness enters blackness thus complicating the idea of races as fixed and static categories. The problem with this analysis of race as a construction is that it misses the element of power and the cost to black professional players when they fail to consciously or unconsciously follow the idiosyncrasies of white men. When the white tutor 'enters blackness' it does not have the same consequences because he controls the cultural environment in which the course takes place, which is part of his heritage. But it is his power and the power of other white men to dictate the performances of black players that leads to a complex relationship between onside racism, that black players see, and an offside form that white men fail to see due to their denial and failure to accept what black men feed back to them about how their feelings in this setting are real. For example, at the end of this course the white students shouted 'hooray, hooray' and began to mock the white tutors. This is an indication of the unthinking ease with which they can take risks that black players have to think about. They can be free to act in this manner without consequences. This form of parody by white men of white men is both public and permissible, leaving black players having to assess more carefully how they take part in these scenes and the implications for their chances of passing the course. Ultimately, only one of them passed the course.

The black players then expressed their feelings when the white players went, reflecting a freedom of being alone, safe and in control, reinforced by the way they end up singing the famous Gloria Gaynor song '*We will survive*'. The song also reflects their travel and survival through the mysterious and contradictory ways of being assessed as black men trying to obtain a coaching qualification. This pressure is best reflected in this comment from the black ex-player who was forced to take his glasses and cap off:

> I feel this course is just a mirror image of the personalities who run it. They are backward thinking, racists and colonialist, you have a better chance of passing the course in America. Working class and black people have no chance on this course. (Black course member)

The anger of this comment reflects how he linked what went on in the coaching course to the age of colonialism, and the way he was treated by white men who he sees as behaving in the same way as white men acted to undermine and discriminate against black men in this historical period. He makes very important links to how his feelings reflect a larger picture of the power white men have in wider society, which filters into the control they use in the coaching setting. One implication of this comment is that it can lead black men to conveniently portray white men as 'all the same', always behaving in this manner in this institutional setting, so their individual capacity to exercise racism is disregarded. Thus it is important to see the individual encounters between black ex-players and white course members and tutors as revealing different dynamics and different outcomes.

Black ex-players have to translate the unconscious acts of white men without being involved in the design of the course – in a situation where their own experiences and values are not represented. They are alienated from any democratic process to challenge the rationale behind how white tutors judge them as they do not have the opportunity to define themselves and their role within the organizational culture of the coaching qualification.

This alienation is felt most particularly when in the role of the researcher and participant you cannot protect or advocate on behalf of black ex-players whilst on the course, when you have to collude with these processes of discrimination just to see race exclusion taking place. For example, although I was fortunate to witness this part of an institutional oragnizational culture in motion, I watched with profound despair the way in which black players had to accept the unsubtle tone of the white tutors and the unconscious forms of racist marking they had to endure. Witnessing the experiences of black players created an anxiety about the cost of having to be ethical and the actual tensions between when to observe and when to intervene when seeing the failure of black players to assert themselves to challenge racism and the lack of honesty from the white tutors about their racism. This issue of honesty is extremely important because you realize, when you are watching the course take place, the implications of coming out and telling the participates that you are actually researching them. This is far more difficult for a black researcher for two reasons. Firstly, because you fear that white men will act in similar ways as they have been seen to act towards black ex-players on the course, insensitive and unable to see how they act out the privilege of being white. More significantly, it becomes less easy to observe how white men act and it becomes more difficult to see how they manipulate this environment to meet their needs. Secondly, it places more pressures on black ex-players who have to face another form of judgement in terms of surviving in this environment knowing that the presence of a black researcher may lead white men to either be more patronizing or more oppressive. The opportunity to witness at first hand the pressures the environment places on black men, and the pressures white men place on black men, is taken away. I remember asking one of the black students if he would tell me about his experiences on the course. Surrounded by his white tutor and other white course members, he whispered 'I'll talk to you later in my room' (interview with black course member, 1994).

The opportunity never arose. He failed the course. The discomfort he felt in being one of the few black players performing in this setting could not be vocalized, as he could not talk with any freedom about the problems of racism he faced in this setting – especially the racism that takes place at the heart of the coaching qualifications – and then expect white men to be impartial if they are seen to be acting in a very exclusive manner and if this is commented on. Being in dual role as a black participant and observer had exposed me to the levels of deference black candidates had to adopt to obtain a qualification. I realized I was in a similar position because to challenge racism meant losing the privilege of seeing white men act naturally, uninhibited by my presence, whilst I had to constantly consider how much my own credibility was being eroded by selling out for the benefit of this project. I had to constantly work out whether it was worth shutting my mouth whilst being abused by an environment and the actions of individual white men just to show how racism operates inside soccer. I became locked in a series of dramatic internal reckonings. My role of being a researcher and participant at the same time was called into question when I had to do a session myself. It was tested again on another level when considering whether it was important to gain a top coaching qualification or whether it was more important to observe racism take place as just another participant.

This tension between being a participant and being an observer came alive on one occasion. I had just finished a session after injuring my back and was in great pain. The white tutor refused to give me more time to rest and forced me to go on and do my coaching topic. I confronted the tutor in the canteen. He was surrounded by a number of his white colleagues just at the start of the queue. I asked him why he had forced me to go on when he knew I was injured. He then suddenly grabbed hold of me, pushed me into a corner and was just about to punch me in the face. I put my hand up to protect myself, and his friends pulled him off me. I realized that his authority had been threatened publicly, but he had let his personal feelings, his own personal strategy, come to light, a violent and physical response in the company of his white friends. This moment is a classical example of what it means to be a black researcher, to see the extreme levels white men will go to control the outsider. I realized at this very moment that simply to observe on one level and not report the incident would contradict my own complaints about the failure of other black players to report or to do anything about the ways in which they have been treated by white personnel. I was approached by the senior white tutor the day after this incident who told me that an investigation had been carried out.

Offside Racism in the Classroom

The changes in the full licence course have led to the whole coaching and management structure of courses in English soccer moving towards integration with the European system. In recent years this has led to major changes in the structures of coach education and the introduction of a new generation of courses, involving much more academic and classroom-based work. The major revamp has involved a move away from the field to the need to complete an increased number of hours in the classroom studying the following components in the form of the UEFA.A conversion course and the pro licence:

- preparing for management;
- self-organization;
- time management;
- managing people;
- counselling, communication;
- football food;
- football fitness

The classroom setting becomes the scene of a new drama. Additional hours are required and high-profile coaches and managers are involved, during many residential-based lectures, group work and a range of different types of assessments involving all aspects of football. In general the climate and culture of the setting is very similar. The Umbro attire is now replaced by tracksuits or suits worn in the classroom. As with the field-based work there are few black ex-players, especially on the pro licence course given the small numbers of black ex-players who have become coaches and managers and who are invited onto these courses. On the first day the lecturer talks in great detail about the importance of CVs in accessing jobs in the market of coaching and management, dressed in a blue suit and standing in front of a number of Premiership and First Division managers. There is a dispute in one corner of room as this idea is contested. Sitting next to a black ex-player in the classroom who is getting increasingly restless, I overhear him saying: 'What a load of shit, do you think anybody in this room has ever got a job by filling out a CV? Do you really think any of these top white managers is going to respond to my CV when they are more than likely to give the job to their friends?' (Darren Smith).

Darren's comment highlights the contradiction between the theory of the course and the actual realities for black ex-players confronting the way that white men talk about the need for roles without reference to the hidden forms of networks that more crucially determine how white men seem to hold onto these roles. Ironically, later on in the course the theme of networking was promoted as the single most important means of getting a job. It is actually seen as more important than the coaching qualification or the need for CVs, thus making qualifications redundant as the prerequisite to equality. This is reflected in the following definition of networking taken from the section on the 'Preparing for management' role:

Networking

This refers to the activity of building up networks of contacts with individuals involved in the Football Profession who can potentially provide help and support for, and be involved in, the management role. If you list the people whom you know now or whom you have had contact with in the past, it is likely that you will discover you already have a network of friends and acquaintances in the field. It is important to be pro-active in networking and think about whom you would like to meet and who would potentially be an important source of support and advice. Knowing a network of people in the game is important in obtaining employment. They may be able to provide information about posts which are (becoming) available or to act as referees and comment on your personality and experience. Networking occurs naturally as your range of colleagues grows: however there are ways of improving your networking skills.

This issue of needing a referee to comment on one's personality and experience involves a powerful exercise of discretion and almost obliges you to beg to convince somebody to give you a good character reference as an opening regardless of any competence based upon qualifications. Networks thus create the illusion they are open for all candidates, whilst concealing the powers that define and construct how these networks function in reality to enable people to get a favorable recommendation and a job. Consequently the real issue concerns the performances appropriate for entering and succeeding on a network, the kind of acts that are necessary to form the right associations. These are often unspoken and embodied, which may mean black ex-players may have to act in a variety of different ways, as reflected in the following definition of impression management taken from Goffman (1956):

> The overall impression you create as an individual and as a professional is extremely important. The things you do and say and help people to understand what you are about, they create an impression of you as a person. Learning to manage that impression is also an important part of preparing for, and building being successful in, the management role.

This comment suggests that there are formulas that help men bond and form within a range of informal personal relationships, to effect the correct performance geared to an 'access card' issued and stamped by predominantly white men who control both the entry to the network and renewal status. Black ex-players see these networks operating in a number of ways organized by and through white personnel, in closed and open environments where they have little influence. In the context of the classroom the performance needed to become part of a network effectively is revealed through the subtle powers of white men to define and approve how to act and how to talk. For example, during an afternoon discussion on networking the tutor asks what the important elements are in terms of communication. A black student puts up his hand up and says: 'I think it's important to try and work with people from different areas of the country, especially with more Asian people coming into the country we need to find out how to work in the best way possible' (Black course member interview). The white tutor delivering the lecture looks stunned. He responds to the black player saying, 'Yeah, I am not sure what you mean, but let's move on.' His disapproval is shown by the embarrassing tone of his voice, a puzzled expression and a stunned disbelief, similar to the negative responses given towards black men in the coaching field where it is clear that a response is not the answer expected. A prominent ex-England coach puts his hand up and the tutor smiles and invites him warmly to make a contribution giving a positive wave of his hand. The coach puts his glasses at the end of his nose and talks in a loud and clear manner: 'You see at our club we have more and more players coming from the continent, more top players from the continent, there are many cultural and language barriers, and to get the best out of them we need to integrate them into our style of doing things' (Steve Bridges). The strong nodding amongst many of the white managers (like the nodding dogs head in the back of a car) captures a unique but unconscious style of social approval, contrasting with the negative reception given to the previous remark from the black student. It is preconscious and embodied in this simple act of a head movement as an indicator of how white men value each other in and outside the football context. This demonstrates how white men working within a pre-coded masculine mode undermine the contribution of black men and their knowledge base.

Unlike on the football field, where white men demonstrate more public forms of racism made transparent by the recipient, black ex-players, in the classroom racism becomes less detectable, because it is featured in these more subtle processes of communication between the white tutor and the white course members. In the football field, black players can more evidently imitate the roles demanded by white tutors, although how their performance is privately marked is difficult to evaluate. In the classroom there is no formal assessment as to what is considered a good or a bad answer. It is based on how white men validate their experiences through unspoken moments. The classroom represents the link of other external social and private locations and relationships where white men develop a sense of being free to simply act white. It is this that is at the centre of the problems black players face. Because the conditions and patterns of familiarity are not rooted in their histories, they fail to be actively involved in the necessary networks and impression management.

Cheers, the Bar and Offside Forms of Racism

The movement of the participants from the field and the classroom into one of the more symbolic spaces of white male masculinity, the bar, reflects, I believe, a football culture that has a special reference for very visible, but unconscious racist acts through intoxication. It is a crude rhetorical form experienced by black players who keep it undisclosed for the benefit of their career development. The bar is thus a secret point for white men and their networks to nurture particular forms of inclusion, illustrated in the following example taken from the UEFA A conversion course, during which the white ex-England coach who made the remark about players integrating into the English game, retired to the bar. In the middle of the bar most of the white participants assembled around this white coach, drinking lager whilst listening intently to his amusing anecdotes about his coaching days. The laughter became louder and louder like a session at speaker's corner as more and more managers and coaches gravitated towards this comical performance. One or two of the black ex-players situated themselves on the edge of this process, and were subjected to a number of racist parodies as this white coach continued, unaffected by their presence:

You know I am standing in the coaching session trying to explain to this black geezer but nothing is going through. I say fuck it lets call it day, so all the players get changed and shower. This thick black guy gets into the shower and comes out and I tell you he has the biggest 'dick' I have ever seen in my life, and if he had tripped over he could have beaten the pole-vault record. (Steve Bridges, first team coach 1996)

The punch line was accompanied by an explosive laughter that reverberated throughout the room, as the white tutors in the corner of the room shared in the laughter, almost implicitly validating these racist caricatures.

In this room white men shared in the demeaning of the black body, as on the plantation field. These references to genitals, size and intelligence were revisited in this public declaration of a gross lack of respect for black men. The laughter was important to the consensus and showed that black men, irrespective of the stereotype being expressed through humour, are perceived by white men as essentially different. The location is vital to understanding the switch in white male behaviour, because, in the bar area, under the influence of drink, somehow racism is not taken as seriously so the underlying degrading of black men is lost. But I think drink removes the white man's guard, so we see through this Dutch courage the emergence of his true feelings towards black men. As observed in the first chapter, Basso (1979) argued that the truth is often expressed as a joke. What is also revealed is the kind of conduct black men in this setting have to accommodate when they have to present themselves in situations where white men are behaving badly. Consequently the calm but dismissive response from the black players shows a propensity to accept these remarks since failure to do so might affect their chances of breaking into these networks. They have to assess whether it is possible to speak out and risk the possibility of being seen as too sensitive to take a joke in this new zone of whiteness.

As a participant and a course member I could observe white men being white men without being inhibited about my role as a researcher who is black in this white male space from a personal and professional perspective. I could take the risk of speaking on behalf of the other black men who were unable to express anger at being disrespected. This is shown in two further examples.

On one occasion I was sitting in the bar surrounded by 25 white professional footballers, who had been drinking all evening in the corner. The light was dim, glasses half empty, the talk revolved around old playing experiences and the recollection of famous drinking encounters told over and over again. I sat quietly, the only black man in the room. One of the members of the group came up to me, slurring his words and breathing stale lager. He asked me if I had any drugs. I said no and that I didn't smoke. He responded: 'You don't smoke? You're joking! Most Rasta men with locks smoke' (White course member).

I contained my emotional response of hostility by checking my feelings of disdain about how this white man was constructing a stereotypical image of me in front of an audience of other white men. I had to respect his right to be offensive in order to watch live a crude, onside form of racism, so as to understand the rationale behind his comment – how his image of a ganga-smoking Rasta connected to his wider social world that related to his ideologies of black men in the game. By opening up these acts, which become concealed before an audience of white men, we can see the development of a white masculine culture that makes assumptions that black men with locks, wherever they are, sell drugs, irrespective of the fact that they are trying to complete a course to gain a coaching qualification. That black men despite their qualification, experience or status in the game carry this legacy of being drug dealers and in one moment can be relegated back to these stereotypes, that they are simply seen as one-dimensional characters, illustrates the pathologies expressed in Chapter 1. To enlighten these white men and give them feedback to enable these forms of racism to become conscious as the first stage of changing their stereotypes of black men was not my aim. My mission as a black researcher was to access white men acting in a variety of 'their' ways, by being silent, to face abuse as a routine aspect of the project, to allow this moment just to happen without any intervention.

More crucially, as Bourdieu (1999) observed, we may question whether it is possible to talk about racism and translate it as a real concrete substance:

> Can racist remarks be reported in such a way that the person making them becomes intelligible, and can it be done without legitimating racism? How can we do justice to the remarks without entering into the reasoning, without accepting that reasoning? (Bourdieu, 1999: 623)

This issue of making sense of racism and making the perpetrator intelligible is both a political and an emotional dilemma that must be qualified by declaring one's position and one's feelings, especially in this rare context in which black researchers are trying to explain the behaviour of white men. The most important issue for me has been to declare my fears of my perspective on racism being perceived as rhetorical. It is a fear made real by the themes outlined in the introduction in which white men dismiss the black voice, so the black voice itself becomes unintelligible by stating what seems to be the obvious in that white men do not like being observed and their racism being made sense of. This issue of the black gaze, particularly the black male gaze, being too close but closeness being an important analytical privilege is reflected in this next encounter, which took place in the bar after an incident in the coaching field.

A white man was being assessed during one of his coaching practices, which was going badly, and he grew angrier as it deteriorated. He picked up his assessment sheet and marched away from the assessor after glancing at his marks; by the stern look in his face he was extremely disappointed. At the end of the day when all the candidates have done their session it is customary to go to the bar. I had formed a friendship with this white man during the course and had confided in him on occasions about racism in the system. On many occasions he seemed sympathetic towards the problems facing black students being assessed in an all-white environment. He walked over to me in the bar, looked directly into my eyes and said: 'Who do you think you are some kind of black Hitler? All you are interested in doing is getting jobs for black people like yourself' (White course member).

His comments made me feel vulnerable to the suspicion of white students about my hidden role on the course. More painfully it was the manner of being crucified in public, being denounced as the 'black Hitler' that made me feel I was being made responsible for his poor remarks. I was his scapegoat. It illustrated the possible fear white men have about being seen to act white, and the problems of making their racist remarks intelligible, as a possible form of projection, which has a historical base in that black men are not important in their world, and politically they should not have a position, and should not be allowed to advocate on behalf of the black cause. Consequently the presence of a black man opens up the reservations of white men, more specifically the fears of jobs going to black men, thus threatening this white man's control and position in this industry.

The bar is an important but discreet and powerful feature of the coaching establishment, an intrinsic part of white male culture. It represents an informal recruitment agency with hierarchical forms of white male power where black men have to both read and study the form. On entry to the bar tutors place themselves in one of the corners, separating themselves from the students, as one important class formation. The few students privileged to enter this space are those who have developed a relationship with the tutors before the start of the course. These class divisions are split further into subgroups of players who already have jobs, but have been sent on the course to obtain the qualification and a subgroup of players who will arrogantly state that they don't need the qualification. The bar thus becomes an important place where students negotiate and where players can market themselves, a form of prostitution in which jobs are exchanged in a space where the selection criteria are based upon friendships, being secure within a relationship with another white man.

Black ex-players, trying to break into these networks in the context of the bar, need to have built up friendships with white players before the course. It is imperative that they assess how these networks operate and the cultures that determine the point of entry.

Let me illustrate this point by referring to a moment when one of the black ex-players was sitting in the corner of the bar drinking an orange juice, surrounded by several white ex-players drinking lager. One of the white men asked: 'who is buying the second round?' The black ex-player offers to do so and buys himself a pint of lager like the rest of the ex-players, as his first attempt to force his way into this network. In speaking to the black ex-player the next day I was interested to find out the experience of being part of this process in the bar area with a number of white men and their power to shape his dependency to get a job. He sat still for a moment and a wide grin appeared on his face, he looked me in the eye and responded as if he was going to make a public announcement:

> You know, I felt like a total outsider, although we laughed together and had a drink, it was hard being there. What was strange about it was these were the same people who were part of my group and when I had my session they did not want to work for me and I even heard one of them say let's make sure he gets a bad mark. (Black course member)

I use the comment to illustrate the barriers that exist between black and white ex-players, the possibility to feel included, but also the potential to feel excluded, at the very same moment when sharing a drink, and that the two emotions can operate at the same moment.

The fact is that white men can unconsciously conspire to dent the prospect of the outsider, until they can demonstrate meeting their acceptance criteria. These criteria can change dependent on the feelings of the individuals, to the extent that the group can fragment into those who will accept black men and those who will not want to accept them. The experiences of black ex-players make visible the culture of the environment where white men reproduce their histories and reveal the sacrifices needed to be seen as competent, not as a coach but in assimilating at different levels dependent on the different perceptions of white men involved in this process.

What becomes apparent is that the more informal the setting, the more difficult it becomes for black ex-players to deconstruct how white men operate. The distinction between onside and offside forms of racism becomes blurred because of black ex-players' distance from the comfort zones, the physical spaces and emotional places in which white men can be themselves. Thus the capacity to enter into these comfort zones measures the ability of black ex-players to compromise, to develop different masks to deal with the different forms of racism that they face, from the pitch, to the classroom, to the arena of the bar. The mask loses its effectiveness because white men behave in contradictory ways and the criteria for being included become more obscure to the extent that it is impossible to predict the best way to collude and find a place amongst white men. Black ex-players express feelings of isolation and injustice, which reflects the fact that they do not have the same access as white men to jobs as coaches and managers.

More critically despite the recent moves in the governing body of soccer, the Football Association, to recommend and impose qualifications as essential to getting a job inside football, the newly introduced pro licence is ironically by invitation only, and only open to certain coaches and managers. This process of invitation is open to discretion and preferential access and reinforces a major problem in the game at present in that most of the black ex-players who have become coaches and managers are located in the second and third divisions, trying to work through a system that closes its doors to them by the introduction of this new system. The last few years have seen this new system of accessing qualifications being exploited and abused unofficially in a racist manner. This occurs in two ways: firstly, by the fast-tracking of white players – the Football Association has given priority to a number of ex-England players to give them a short cut to the UEFA A level and on to the pro licence, with no rationale about how these individuals are selected except to safeguard against the lack of white English men able to take on the national England job. Secondly, this rush to get white players qualified empowers white men to use a new type of network in which they cannot be criticized for not having the necessary qualification for becoming coaches and managers. Whilst there have been a few black players who have benefited from this new fast-track system, none of them is presently located in the technical department of the Football Association advocating on behalf of the needs of black players.

It is important to mention the implications for the black players working at semi-professional and grassroots levels. These levels are now far removed and becoming more distant from the top qualifications needed to get a job inside soccer. There are very few UEFA A licence holders and coach educators at this level. They are now well below white professional players and below black professional players, and they are nowhere near the locations where important decisions are being made about their ability to work inside soccer. Ironically, they are unable to compete with their white male counterparts who are also moving ahead of black professional players into coach education and beyond. Unfortunately the sporting industry has decided to look at the mentoring needs of this community to these stages, without paying attention to how the structure of the coaching qualifications works in favour of the white male experience. The central issue here is not the problem of getting on a coaching course, but how important these qualifications are in breaking the glass ceiling in terms of actually getting a job as a coach or a manager in English soccer.

Despite all the barriers that black men face in getting qualified and surviving in a culture that is dominated by white men in both the structure and content of the course, the crucial issue is: does it really make a difference? There is a danger that what takes place in English society operates inside English soccer. The overly qualified black player has spent his time getting these paper qualifications but not gaining the sufficient experience of doing the job. However, without the qualifications players face criticism for being underqualified. They fall between these two accusations, whilst being measured and assessed by criteria that have nothing to do with qualifications.

I feel that it is important to end this chapter by comparing the world of qualifications inside soccer to their value to the outside social world, where issues of overqualification also arises, and the world where what you act like and who you know is much more important. Sadly in the area of research, writing and publication the issue of creditability through qualifications is a myth, especially in the attempt to get the black gaze in the institutions of sport heard and respected, without being seen as too close.

–3–

Onside and Offside Forms of Racism in the Transition into Coaching and Management

After completing a coaching qualification it is assumed that doors open, access is equitable for both black and white men to get jobs as coaches and managers, as discussed in the last chapter. I followed the progress of twelve soccer players who had retired from the game and were seeking these positions: five white ex-players and seven black ex-players. They were asked about how they saw their future and their perceptions of race inequality in the transition into coaching and management. Their accounts, in which these ex-players represent themselves and their social position, were explored using Portelli's (1991) approach of considering the form of the narrative, which 'allows us to recognize the interests of the tellers, and the dreams and desires beneath them'. What is useful about this approach is that it makes the truth or falsity of the narrative of secondary importance; it is what the narrative reveals about the values of the speaker that is crucial. The values I analyse can be found in Ruth Frankenberg's (1993) study of the way that white women orientated themselves towards issues of race and racism as revealed in the personal accounts of the people in her sample. She identifies two contrasting patterns: 'race cognizance' and 'power evasiveness'. She suggests:

> Race cognisance articulates explicitly the contradiction that racism represents: on one hand it acknowledges the existence of race inequality and white privileges and, on the other it does not lead to ontological and essential differences in order to justify inequality or explain it away. By contrast the colour – and power evasiveness repertoire is organized away efforts to represent or evade the contradiction. Race cognisance in this sense generated a range of political and essential questions about white complicity with racism. (Frankenberg 1993: 160)

The idea of 'race cognizance' captures the potential for a critical understanding to emerge from white men in relation to racism, while, 'power evasiveness' identifies the ways that they create a form of racism by denying any responsibility for their power as white men. My sample of five white ex-soccer players enabled me to examine how they devoid themselves of a race identity, to use their power without any links to their masculinity. I compared the narratives of the black ex-players to see how they deal with their relationships with white men through the changing faces of racism: from the playing field, to the coaching qualification to the move into coaching and management. These pathways reflect their power to adapt to and adjust the system in relation to their own personal needs and their cultural experiences. It is by focusing on the changes in the narratives of these ex-players that their cognizance of their race and their power as men is influenced by their individually different experiences within the system.

Year One

White Players: Meritocracy and Hard Work
I start here with Gareth West, born in England with Irish parents; he played for the youth team, reserve team and for the first team. During our first interview he talked about his professional career from Queens Park Rangers to his last club, Luton Town. At this stage of his career he had completed his UEFA A coaching badge and he had one year left on his contract as a player at Luton Town. He was beginning to come to terms with what it means to finish his playing career and find a new identity inside football:

> It would be the saddest day ever, I love the game, and I absolutely love the game. I couldn't accept it that age is catching up with me. From the age of 32, I have prepared myself for ending my career, that's why I got my full badge, so if I go for a job against somebody who has not got it I might be a step nearer getting it. (Gareth West)

Gareth mourns the loss of his status as a professional player, which seems to motivate him to find a new position in the system, whilst a coaching qualification enables him to feel that he will have a better chance of getting a job as a coach. Thus he colludes with the myth that the qualification represents a system that is progressed through in stages, similar to the stages of becoming a professional footballer, as illustrated in his next comment:

> If a job did come it would have to be in stages, may be youth team level, may be assistant manager and then first team level, that is my aim in an ideal world. You have to deal with the chairman, all the directors; you have to deal with the contracts. I would have to learn to manage it. I think you would have to distance yourself from players, I think it would be easier to go to another club and do it. (Gareth West)

Gareth promotes a transition into a system that is linear, which he has to pass smoothly through on route to becoming a manager. His fear in having to confront new personnel such as directors and the chairman that he was accountable to as a player is without any sense of race differentials. Gareth does not have to think about inferiority or needing to change his behaviour to be accepted by white men. He can manage these new relationships, especially now that he is becoming an authority figure in relation to other players with the need for distance, thus reproducing the coldness he has experienced. More crucially, he begins to construct a system where he finds a place with other white men who will support his role and his identity as a coach. He thus produces a form of 'power evasiveness' because as a white man he does not have to think about being different, in terms of his race identity in moving from a player to a coach. He is able to operate in an atmosphere where the privileges of being a white man are never challenged, an unconscious position of race superiority that is never made transparent similar to the position adopted by Les Jackson, the second white player in my sample.

Jackson was born in London to Welsh parents. He had also worked through the system, spending his career at Watford Football Club. He also had completed his UEFA A coaching badge and perceives a system where hard work is rewarded by a job as a coach:

> I went straight to Watford Football Club, and I played for one club, and then had to retire. I was advised to give up the game at 28 years of age. I was already working with the young kids; I wanted to go into coaching and management particularly on the youth side. It is difficult there are only so many jobs, I would like the opportunity to become first team manager, jobs are hard to come by and they are harder to keep. (Les Jackson)

In this comment Les's aspirations of becoming a coach and holding onto his position is justified by entrenching himself in the system he is in, his home, the club he played for most of his life. He creates a system where jobs are sought and held, where access operates by having to move instrumentally through the club structure to be rewarded. His power as a successful coach evolves by doing everything he can to minimize the likelihood of losing control of the environment where he's placed as an irremovable figure. He believes in a system where, once he has done the work necessary to break in, he has to maintain his role and his status where jobs are not based on any format of equality. Unlike Gareth he thinks that going on a coaching course does not guarantee a job or progression through the system; the system operates by ensuring that there is nobody around to replace you. It operates through being discreet, watching your back and ensuring that you are not vulnerable, a meritocracy based upon being best at seeing and removing any competition. Les, at this point of entry, shows a lack of consideration as a white man in participating in a system that is not based on any equitable standards. This luxury of taking one's race for granted and not needing to consider it as an inhibiting factor leads to a confidence and a freedom that enables the next two white players to talk more openly about being able to exploit the system for their own benefits.

Offside Racism as a Form of Self-assurance and Incestuous Networking

Tony Francis was resolute about soccer as the only career he was interested in; he started his playing career at Lincoln, ended it at Wimbledon and played for

England on two occasions. He was part way through his UEFA B coaching badge and was offered a job as the reserve team coach at Wimbledon Football Club having finished his playing days with the club. In Tony's new role he developed a confidence and self-assurance by being so naturally part of a system where he does not have to conceptualize the privileges of being white, of how this leads to a historical form of racism in the recruitment of mainly white men. He can then see his progress as operating through his own motivation, which disguises the fact that he has a head start in this transition as a white ex-player:

> I influenced myself; Football is all I know and all I wish to know. There is no transition into coaching and management no one spoke to me. I've got faith in my own ability and how I work and if I retired and not been offered a job at Wimbledon Football Club, I would have applied elsewhere. I am glad I got a foot on the ladder the opportunity and look upon it as a new career. (Tony French)

Tony like other ex-players feels that they have to exploit other people in the system in order to get a position. Alan Ward was born in London and progressed through the traditional playing system, from youth team to first team player. He had also completed his UEFA A coaching badge. Despite Alan having had a similar playing career, from Queens Park Rangers to twelve years at Arsenal, his position is different from that of the other white players as he already had a management job at Slough Football Club:

> I didn't really make the conscious decision to become a manager. I was assistant manager at Yeovil, but left Yeovil and came back from Hong Kong at the age of 34; I came back to nothing. I did my coaching courses for whatever reason just to give me an option. And I got the job at Slough doing their football in the community. But I want to work as a full-time manager, if you get the opportunity you have gone to take it. (Alan Ward)

Alan, by feeling that he does not have to make a conscious decision about a career in management, or see the need for a coaching qualification, creates a system that depends on how he manipulates it and makes it work for him. He has the privilege of coming back to 'nothing' and still feeling confident that the system can work for him. More specifically he reveals a ruthlessness in taking the chance, similar to the playing field, to be first and put to bed any claim to any democratic process in the transition to becoming a coach or a manager inside English soccer:

> Well, I would like to manage in the Football League. I've got personal ambitions but I think that's something you keep to yourself, if you achieve them nobody needs to know. You got to have ability but it's also who you know, you have got to have networks, if

you don't know people and you haven't got a background it's difficult to get into. (Alan Ward)

In Alan's comment he defends his beliefs about the need for secret networking, revealing again this quality of sheer arrogance that colonizes the system by the way that white men adopt it as their own without thinking about the consequences for others. Wallace Brent begins to capture the ongoing dialectical relationship between the individual and the system. This dialectical process is determined by the quality of one's relationship with other professionals, through which white ex-players perpetuate different levels of being at ease with other white men, revealing a system that can operate on contradictory levels.

Pragmatism and White Male Indifference

Wallace was beginning to see the strategies he had to develop to progress into the institution of coaching. He had moved into soccer late, which he saw as giving him a greater will to succeed. His previous job was as a labourer; he then entered the league scene at twenty-five years of age and did not have the same experience of the playing system as the other white players I interviewed. More crucially, unlike the other white players Wallace's experience of the multicultural context of Crystal Palace and seeing black players experience racism contributed towards the way he perceived the ambiguous ways that individuals move into jobs in the professional cultures of soccer. He is able to connect this ambiguity in relation to his own move-ment, as dependent upon the types of relationships he was able to develop with other white men. Playing professional football was seen as the most important pre-requisite to forming contacts:

> Les James at Charlton most influenced me in terms of going into management. When I was a player at Barnet, Ian Bull took me to Reading as reserve team manager. I am lucky that I do have a manager, who knows I want to become a manager and he's big enough to have me in the background and not worry about me. I know there are defi-nitely managers who don't think like that, that's why a lot of jobs in football go to friends. (Wallace Bren)

Wallace's comment shows that it is the dynamics within these networks that influence how individuals get into coaching and management, how men get on and fail to get on. This is similar to the processes of association in the world outside football. He had to operate in a system that is built on vulnerable men who depend on friendships with other white men who will not take their job, so they stay in the background and can be taken anywhere without threatening one's position. His pathway as a coach is determined by somebody else losing their job, and being mentored, then sponsored in his move into a coaching position. His account shows no awareness of the implications of the way that white men maintain relationships with the same white men to develop these systems of sponsorship. This pattern of white men consistently working with the same white man, as a pattern of mutual comfort, was tested in Wallace's life when Ian Bull was sacked as the first team manager at Reading. The outcome for Wallace was that he had to adopt a more pragmatic approach to his entry and movement, since his plan of taking the job of his friend was disrupted. Unlike the previous four white players, Wallace saw a system where you are dispensable and will not always be guaranteed a job. It is a consciousness that almost borders on recognizing that black players face a different type of pressure in coming into this system, without making Wallace accountable for their exclusion:

> If you're thinking of white chairmen not choosing black players and I think that would only be the case with about 2% of them. I can think of Mark Stephens who was always very together and very smart. I think that some chairmen might be frightened by that, so I don't know if he would get a break. (Wallace Brent)

Wallace's account defines an industry where white chairmen choose black players who will not disrupt the system, but fails to recognize the possibility of two percent of these white men being racist in their decision making represents a form of racism and cannot be considered as just another isolated moment. A pattern emerges where Wallace can see these processes of exclusion but he does not have to think about how racism operates in the context of his own recruitment. He can then avoid having to look at his power or see the privileges he has as a white man in this system that discriminates against black ex-players he was close to in his playing days.

Onside Clarity of Racism, Black Players Trust, Fate and the Disillusioned
The narratives of the black ex-players reflect a conscious form of racism as they become contemptuous of the processes of institutionalized racism that operate in the system in which their white male counterparts fail to see and flag up. For example, Darren Smith was born in Jamaica; he started his career at Wolves and ended his career at Port Vale. He went through the traditional playing system from youth team to first team player, like the white players. In this comment Darren begins to think about a career in coaching, significantly after he has been out of the system for some time:

> It wasn't until a year after finishing playing that I decided to get into coaching or anything like that. I didn't know what the barriers were. One of the things I was afraid of doing was saying I wanted to be a coach and finding out that I couldn't be a coach and that I was a broke layabout. I remember feeling really disappointed when the job at Cambridge came up and Brendon Batson applied for it and he didn't get it. (Darren Smith)

Darren's apprehensiveness about a career as a coach reveals his feelings about a system that does not operate equally for black ex-players because of the mystery of the barriers they confront. More specifically he fears that he will be seen as much more than just another reject, and this will have profound implications for his status outside the football world. He shows a reluctance to declare an interest based upon a suspicion that the black ex-players who have gone before set the precedent of being discriminated against. Darren sees the risk of failure as too severe after a year out the game for him to give up everything for a career that might not happen. It is a barrier that is insurmountable. Darren's apathy about a system that does not offer the same pathways to black ex-players reinforces his fears of being condemned by a form of racism, unconscious to white men, which would have implications for his whole life:

> I've got my Prelim badge and my full badge and I have been told that my name has been put forward by the Professional Footballers Association. But I want to know if my name was put forward when a proper job comes along. I have developed networks I know many players I see players that are my age and who I have got to know, where are these networks, does that mean that they know more people than me? It seems my networks do not get me a job. (Darren Smith)

Darren sees that his networks are not white enough so becomes marginalized by a system that does not take him, as a black man with a coaching qualification, seriously. The frustration for Darren is that he knows he is being excluded but he cannot see how this exclusion is taking place, it remains 'invisible', especially when he sees white players progressing through their networks that become 'white only zones'. Darren realizes the limits of his power as a black man by pinpointing the privileges of white ex-players to be in a system where they do not think about their powers. He thus left completely demoralized, but having the greatest insight into how the system works unofficially.

The second black player in my sample also illustrates this feeling of a lack of power through his distrust of the system in which white men are so prominently in control. David Boyce was born in London and also went through the same system of playing, starting within the Youth team at Manchester City. He finished his playing career at Cambridge United after a long spell at Tottenham. He felt unsure about staying in the game because he felt that he had been treated like a child and discouraged by the white managers he had worked under in both his professional and social life:

> Ideally there are things I would like to do outside of the game, before wanting to come back into football. Football has become a game of who you know, whoever the manager is his number two is usually somebody he has met via football or played with or played under. We are now getting to the first generation of black players retiring, making the

first stage on the ladder as coaches, what we really need is a black person on the board of a Football Club. (David Boyce)

David's thoughts about a life outside the game reflects a precariousness about a profession based on chance and without a clearly structured equitable career path. Consequently, to give David a better chance there is a need for black representation right up to the level of chairman to equal up the stakes and to advocate on his behalf so he can actually rely on somebody in a system in which qualifications don't matter. He realizes he needs someone who can influence the recruitment procedure and give him some power as a black man and remove the suspicion of same race recruitment. He recognizes the limited importance of a coaching qualification in a situation where he would be less likely to need one if he was white and had been a famous player.

David returned to the importance of his skin colour as he approached retirement, seeing that he was being recognized not as a player but as a black man, at a time when the system finds it easier to accommodate white ex-players.

Exploiting Offside Racism through White Patronage

The next two black ex-players understand and respond to a system where their power is enacted in the way they negotiate their entry and work alongside white men in the system. The power that white men have over black men in this system is revealed in my interview with Ian Harris. He was born in Yorkshire, and went through the traditional playing system, starting his career at Leeds United and ending it after a bad knee injury at Brighton:

> For the ratio of black players at my time it was about 1 to 20 white players, you can't imagine a lot of black players waiting around, thinking well I had a good career, let me do something else now. I don't really want the hazard of being a manager. It may take a black millionaire to buy a club before a black person will be successful. (Ian Harris)

Ian realizes that the chance of progressing to the level of a manager is unlikely due to black ex-players being significantly outnumbered by white players. A psychology of racism leads him to allocate this space as the white man's property, believing that white men control management, and that this can only be challenged if black personnel are already in the system. This position is extremely close to how racism operates in other institutional settings, through lack of black representation, which suggests that the world of sport is similar to society due to a lack of black political power in white structures. Consequently, Ian's career is always dependent upon being selected by a white man who may unconsciously select him as his assistant manager without reference to race:

I haven't applied for any jobs it's always been word of mouth. John Bless wanted me and said would I like to work the reserve team at Bristol Rovers. There was no formal application for reserve team manager and I was then sacked at Bristol Rovers and John Bless was at Bristol City, again it was more or less a phone call about working with him again. (Ian Harris)

For Ian the system works in exactly the same way that it does for white men, through his name being circulated and through being 'approached', with very few black men to approach him or with the power to offer him a job. So his career is determined by the patronage of white men and their willingness to trust and select him. Although his work location may change, his position and his power in relation to his white manager may stay the same. His destiny is determined by accepting that, he must 'wait for the call'; he cannot negotiate his role independently within this system because jobs function through knowing men who are white and who expect black men to accept these forms of dependency.

Stephen Bridges, the fourth black player in my sample, sees his power in his relationships with white personnel in a more complicated way. Stephen is of mixed parentage – his father was from Africa, his mother from Ireland – which complicates how he operates between these worlds of race within the social world of sport, which often responds to him politically as black. He came into the game late after completing an engineering degree and had a 13-year career at Tottenham Hotspurs, before finishing at Brentford. Stephen feels the transition into this system is based upon luck and being in the right place at the right time. He also recognizes the advantage that white players have through the luxury of not having to confront racism as players. More importantly, they do not have to consider a career in relation to their identity as white coaches; they do not suffer the ongoing struggles that black ex-players have to face in being forced to look at the connection between their skin colour and their ability as a coach:

First and foremost I see myself as a coach, secondly I see myself as a black coach just the same way as I see myself as a black person. I think in an idea world I would like to see myself as a coach, but I think society determines that difference. And even as a black person it shouldn't be that way and I would probably say to a majority of white people that they shouldn't see it as black and white, they should just see it as a coach. I want to be judged on being a coach and being a good coach. (Stephen Bridges)

Stephen's ability to be seen simply as a good coach without this being linked to any perceptions of him as a black man, despite his mixed race background, is outside his control as he has to come to terms with a society and a football world where he is continually objectified as black first and a coach second. In trying to be accepted as a coach, he sees the danger of being portrayed in a colour-specific way and compared to the white coaches, which limits both his identity and his opportunities in the professional cultures of football.

In Stephen's life, race cognizance operates on two levels. The first level is the way he sees racism taking place in this system that influences his life opportunities. At the second level he has to analyse his own experience of racism and the personal changes he has to consider making in this system compared to other white men:

> I think the changes apply to white coaches, a white coach would have to conduct themselves in a certain management style, his dress code would have to be different, and his approach to his players would have to be different. And the black coach would have to be the same. I think I am building towards the coaching side. There are so many areas to make breakthroughs and you don't know when one is going to come along. (Stephen Bridges)

Stephen's narrative constructs a system in which, despite the same behaviour and dress codes applying to both black and white ex-players, white men assert their progression whilst Stephen defers to a system that works instrumentally in his ambition to gain a job as a coach. This leads to a hierarchy that is racialized, with black players placing themselves as coaches and white ex-players as managers. Consequently, white ex-players don't question their career progression in the same ways as black ex-players, who have to develop a self-awareness about how their race identity affects their position. Stephen, in trying to identify himself as just a coach, still sees how racism operates to deny him the same privileges that white coaches have. The accounts of these four black players show that they understand their lives in this system in a completely different way to the white ex-players. The overriding issue is that a system emerges where black players face having to make a number of sacrifices and compromises that white players do not have to consider.

Waiting for the White Man's Permission

Les Turner came into the professional game very late at the age of twenty-eight, playing for Boston and finishing his professional playing career at Lincoln City. He lived most of his life in the north after coming to England with his parents from Trinidad. He had also completed his UEFA A coaching badge. He reflected on his entry into the system in this comment:

> You must remember I was working all my life, then I went to Grimsby and I had so much time on my hands, so I went into coaching, then I took my full badge. Steve Brimson got the job, he brought me to Lincoln and I played for a year then I took over the Youth Team and was still playing and then I became manager. Steve Brimson got the sack, the chairman asked me to take over for a couple of games. I was a bit surprised to get the job. (Les Turner)

Les moves from being a player to being a coach without having to think about any direct or specific form of racism. He, unlike the other players, has being in a world outside of football, which he can relate to how racism takes place inside football. Ironically his transition occurred at a moment when the white manager who brought him into the club lost his job and it was offered to Les, as his first opportunity in the system. Les's cognizance of race is therefore not connected to an overt form of racism, because of the ordinary way he is introduced into a system that does make reference to his skin colour at this moment of his career. He is able to adopt a colour-blind perspective at a time when he considers he has power in his new position compared to the more colour-specific position adopted by Tony Francis.

Tony was born in Kingston, Jamaica, and came over to England with his parents in his formative years. He also graduated through the youth team to become a professional football player, firstly at Aston Villa and then at Exeter City. He had an ambition to become a coach early in his career, which enabled him to develop an earlier awareness of how the system operates, and the implications for his identity as a black man:

> Whatever circle you're in you should be able to hold a conversation; if you're in a white circle you should be able to hold a conversation with a white person in a proper manner. If I am with my black friends I go into my patois, you have got to keep your identity, I am a black man full stop. I think there is a question mark against you; people look at you in a different light. I don't change, but I tone it down a little bit. If I was dealing with 11 black lads, it would have to be my culture, I would talk to them in that way, like a black man within the framework of the club. (Tony Francis)

Tony perceives that he will firstly and only be accepted as a coach, leading to an aversion to the management office where he will need the white man's permission, creating a race division that becomes internalized. These race divisions influence how he sees he will have to relate in different ways to black and white men within the constraints of his new role as a coach. He sees that a different cognizance of race relationships is needed to respond to the needs of white men within this system, where he makes more conscious changes to adjust to their world, whilst being able to relate to black players more naturally in terms of his actions and his language. Consequently, through this process of self-analysis, he manages his relationships dependent on the race of the personnel with whom he is interacting, unlike the white players in this sample who show no consciousness of having to relate in a two-dimensional way. Tony sees that white men do not appreciate the cultural context in which he works as a black man. He understands that his life is a series of reckonings and comes to see that he operates within a system of black men and a system of white men where there are very few cross-cultural exchanges. He begins to realize that the only way he can survive in this system, as a black man, is to make himself as valuable as possible by working twice as hard. He also then faces the accusation of being seen to be too close to white people, which opens him up to the criticism of 'selling out', in that he always does what white people tell him to do:

> When I go to games I still get people staring at me, but it doesn't bother me, I know there's a lot of black players out there in the game who think I am a bit of a coconut. I was looking at Ruud Gullitt, there's a man who was at the top of his tree and was sacked. What could they do to somebody like me at the bottom, which has no financial clout like he had? So I am making myself as employable as possible. (Tony Francis)

Tony's account shows the political readjustments made within these white structures as he realizes that he is no longer a player but an employee who does not have the same rights as white men or high-profile black players. Tony's loyalty to this system is then tested on two levels, in relation to his allegiance to his white employees and his allegiance to his identity as a black man. He is accused of selling out his race by seeming to act like a white man even through this was not his intention. He then faces the ongoing tension between being subservient to white male authority figures whilst maintaining his identity as a black man.

William Marke's narrative further illustrates the difficulty of maintaining these two images at the point of his transition into the system, his image as a professional and his image as a black man who has not sold out, or let the side down. William was born in London, to Jamaican parents, and had also progressed through the playing system from youth team player, to a first team-playing career that started at Bristol City and finished at Southend. He then became a youth team coach at Leyton Orient before moving to his present position at the Football Association:

> I have never applied for a job that's the case, when you're half-desperate. They phoned me and asked me to apply for the Football Association job. I think it got to a point when they have looked round and looked at what skills people have and who we got, and we haven't got one of those colours, who can do that, has he played. So then it happens that it becomes politically correct. (William Marke)

When William was offered the job as a coach co-ordinator of the south-east region he believed that his transition was influenced by a system where his colour began to matter for the cosmetic face of the organization, to represent the myth of equality and multiculturalism. William feels he can only be accommodated within white men's perception of him if he performs well and on their terms. He must not expose racism in their system. For William the system will not change, because he does not see individual white men wanting or being able to see the need for change for his benefit. He is made to feel that he must accept how the institution is organized or become marginalized, despite the compromises he makes in this period.

In these first sets of narratives the themes that have emerged are the very clear ways in which the white players show no cognizance of themselves as white men and so consequently do not begin to see the power they have. In contrast to the work of Frankenberg (1993) this is not a matter of power evasiveness as white men have no sense of their 'power' as white men in the first place, therefore there is no need to be evasive. The competition between the white men hides a profound sense of being vulnerable around other white men, who have the potential to offer a job and take a job away. What is revealed in these first interviews is that white men are continually assessing how to use other white men, without having to think that these processes of association are the foundations on which a white identity is built. These associations are not extended across the colour-line with black men as they negotiate new relationships of power with white men in a system that operates in polarized ways. This is because it is a system in which white players have had more time historically to develop and instil their ways of doing things, ways that can be discriminatory in the lives of the black players at this point in their careers. Black players begin to see a system that is controlled and dominated by white men, and accept at this time that racism operates by not giving them the same privileges as white men.

In the second interviews I assessed how these themes from the first interviews changed or remained constant – how forms of race cognizance and power evasiveness move in relation to the individual experiences of these twelve players.

Year 2 and Beyond

The Changing Narratives of the White Players Centralizing the Importance of Self

In Gareth West's first narrative he applied himself to a system based on the ethos of hard work, preaching meritocracy through holding a coaching qualification. In this second interview he orientated himself to the need for friendships as instrumental in assisting his transition from playing into a coaching position, putting to bed any belief in the ethos of equality. Gareth was 36 years of age by the time of this interview. His perception of his life in this system now worked in relation to his own individual selfish ambitions:

I wanted to be a professional footballer. I wanted to be a coach and I want to be a manager. I want to manage at the highest level, I don't know where that will be, but I want to be number one and I want to run a football team, the way I want to run it. (Gareth West)

This change in Gareth's narrative, in asserting his career development and the terms in which he saw himself managing, indicates an arrogance and an egotism. This claim to a job centres race superiority again but more discreetly in Gareth as a white man who begins to dominate this industry by new a confidence about taking control. He then relinquishes his contract as a player at Luton and is offered a youth team job with one of his previous managers. Gary's career as a coach is dependent upon another white man looking out for him, as he now begins to see the benefits of having colleagues in the system to open doors. He does not see these relationships with other white men as contributing towards discriminatory outcomes, as exclusive patterns of white men following other white men around the system, as the most natural ways of staying in this industry. Thus Gareth can avoid seeing his actions as contributing towards processes of inequality, or seeing himself as implicated in covert racist practices, so he does not have to take any responsibility for the collective powers of white men in this system:

> I have many black friends, I have many white friends. If one of my black friends applied for the job and I thought it was right, I would give it to them. But chairmen run the clubs. If they want to employ a black manager they will employ a black manager, if he wants to employ a white guy, he will employ a white guy, and for me colour doesn't matter. (Gareth West)

Gareth portrays a system where race does not matter. It is arbitrary so anyone can benefit. Racism is seen as out there and no way linked to him or to white men in higher positions and no way linked to job selections. The implication of Gareth's colour-blind approach to the system is that he can then work as the youth team manager at Queens Park Rangers, complete his UEFA A coaching badge and learn about his new role without being inhibited by having to be conscious of himself as a conspirator of racism.

Since the time of this interview Gareth has remained in his current role as a reserve team coach. He completed his UEFE A license, but still sees the door open as he does his apprenticeship and it is always open to him.

Les Jackson more assertively recognizes the need to use these white networks to progress as his position had not changed since our first interview. He was still the first team coach at Watford Football Club. He also reaffirms his place in a system where he sees his career is determined by developing associations with other white men as intrinsic to football circuits where jobs are advertised informally:

> It gets you known it gets you on the circuit, you get to know other people and then you get to know when the jobs are coming up. I know there's not a lot of black coaches about, may be they don't take an interest in it, but there's Martin, I do think people have got to be prepared to start at the bottom. (Les Jackson)

Les works on the basis of a 'circuit' formed through relationships of familiarity that act as informal recruitment processes. The power of these processes is disguised by the way Les promotes a meroticratic system that functions by players having to work from the bottom upwards. His example of Martin Andrews, his black colleague, falsely implies that black players can move equitably and obtain a position in this system in this way. This disguises the fact that white players are privileged to a 'fast track' through networks and exclusive 'white male-coded circuits' that become self-perpetuating. Les, during the period between interviews, had coached Watford to promotion from the second to the premier division, pointing to a pattern of white men getting into the system and staying there until an opportunity to progress becomes available.

He has lost his job at Watford and stayed out of the game for several years, then he returned after being offered a job as deputy manager at a second-division club, starting again this process of establishing new foundations, the new circle. Obtaining and learning jobs do not depend upon any open system but upon the strength of relationships. This pattern of networking, based upon close intimate relationships, is described more clearly by Tony and Alan, who in the first interview focused on achieving their own personal needs by manipulating the system through developing partnerships.

Offside Racism by Mentoring through Closed White Male Networks

In the case of Tony Jackson networks featured prominently in his current position as the reserve team manager at Wimbledon Football Club, through the way he was nurtured to do the job, through his relationship with his first team manager. The value of these relationships and the role they play in his advancement within the system are underestimated by Tony compared with the importance of completing his coaching qualification:

> I have done the UEFA B course; my next step is to go on to the UEFA A course next summer. I am still running the reserve team and I am working with Joe Stevens the manager. I leave home at 8.30 am, get to the training ground at about 9.20 am, see who's available, who's injured, who's not, and then coach my reserve team. In the afternoon get some of the youngsters and do some individual work. Then once or twice a week I will watch a game and watch the game on a Saturday. (Tony Jackson)

Tony's comment begins to shape a system by working alongside other white men, gaining more confidence and more of an identity as a coach than he would through gaining a coaching qualification. It is through these routines and contacts, which take place in the setting of a football club, that Tony is able to create his pathway into a job. The importance of being a white man is coded silently by his association with other white men, which becomes exclusive and is never acknowledged as an intricate part of bonding and identity formation. Tony's identity as a coach is based upon having a close and ongoing contact with Brain Hall, his first team coach, who helps him cope with the demands of the system. This enables Tony to consolidate his role in a familiar space, as part of a team where he is valued for being a white man amongst other white men without this recognition of being similar needing to be openly registered. Tony's role within this team is consolidated by observing other white team members at work during moments where he does not have to confront the pressures of whether or not he fits in or he shares easiness about being around them. Whilst Tony works in this company he can progress towards a management position through these behind the scenes processes without having to feel he is doing any thing unjust:

> I am quite happy where I am, I wouldn't go anywhere. Basically I sit here, observes the manager Joe and the other coaches and hopefully learns from them. But I think I have become a stronger person, more adaptable and more flexible, your learning every day. (Tony Jackson)

Like the other white men, he can move on. He goes with his manager to another London club where he situates himself for a number of years until his senior loses his job and he again waits for the call to re-establish this working relationship. Comparing Tony's informal use of his networks to that of Alan's orientation to the system as waiting for his networks to provide access to a management job reaffirms an approach where their progress is not solely related to good management skills. Alan's unwillingness to accept that white players have a better chance of becoming managers and staying in the game leads to a covert form of racism in which he does not have to feel guilty for the way that this form of exclusion operates as factor in giving him advantages over black players: 'I haven't got an issue whether it's a black or a white player. If I was with a professional club I would take Paul Davis with me he's a black guy. I am surprised in this day and age we are actually talking about this issue' (Alan Ward).

Alan's race-neutral approach represents an aversion to seeing how racism operates in the system, which enables him to continue to use his strategy of being secretive, which increases his power to establish networks that exclude non-white men. The outcome is the freedom of being in a system where he does not expect to apply openly with other candidates, even his good friend Paul Davis for a job, although he can assume that Paul is not a victim of this process: 'I haven't applied for any jobs; I don't see myself applying for anything. In terms of networks, well I have got quiet a good network, I know a lot of people in the game, and I know a lot of people in the pro game' (Alan McDermott).

The comment raises an ethical problem that I continually faced regarding how much I could influence the race cognizance of white men like Alan, drawing their attention to the way networks develop as white-only recruitment agencies.

Throughout our relationship over this one-year period, he was suspicious when responding to questions that sought to make him accountable for his position as a white man. The possibility of looking at the issues of race and masculinity was blocked continually by his unwillingness to talk about how his role and power as a coach were influenced specifically by his race and his gender. He became closed and distant as he only wanted to respond to questions about his work and his need to use his networks of friends to get a job as a coach. His refusal to acknowledge racism in the system, which I detected in both his tone of voice and his negative responses concerning racism in the system highlights the fact that, in this white man's imagination I represented a troublemaker, creating ideas of race inequalities of which his world was unconscious. I realized that my presence as a black man could not convert his implicit understanding of racism to a tangible ownership of how race equality operated in his life. His reluctance to see the realities of racism was exposed by his repetitive patterns of talk: 'I don't know' 'I haven't seen' and 'I don't think it is a problem'. This theme of denial also resonated from Tony's and Alan's narratives, which contributes unarguably towards a sense of them being 'worthy' of their position, which is more recognized and validated as a point of entry than the status of having a coaching qualification. Ironically, at the end of this period Alan had not made the type of progress he expected; he had not made it into the premier league. The fact that white men do not always benefit from white networks needs to be understood in relation to the specific processes, qualities and characteristics contained within the network, which do not always work in the same ways for all white men.

Wallace Brent's narrative begins to disrupt the assumption that the relationships between white men working with other white men will naturally lead to a job and being included inside the system.

White Men Adjusting to White Men's Exclusion

Wallace's second interview reflected the specific local problems of white men surviving in a system where they have to work with other white personnel, thus disrupting the fantasy that they always get on with each other. For Wallace, his inability to progress in this system was not based upon race differences, but having to work with somebody who was totally new to his life at Reading Football Club and who might have been involved in his eventual exclusion from this system. To survive, Wallace abided by the club demands to work with a new management team of white men, as the people he depended on were no longer around. Unlike the other white players, he accepted the formal rules of the industry, knowing he was not involved in the new implicit rules enforced by the new regime, and would not be until he could regain a position to work again with somebody he would be comfortable with where he would be back in control:

I haven't applied for any jobs, once I serve my apprenticeship in this job, and then I get a job with a Premiership club or as an assistant manager. In the next year I will complete my UEFA A logbook, I see myself seeing out my contract, learning from Harry Burns in the next 2 years. (Wallace Brent)

Wallace, unlike the four other white players in my sample, showed a cognizance of himself not fitting in with the demands of his new colleagues. This awareness was not connected to him being a white man, but resulted from him seeing his life in a system that did not always operate in the way he constructed it. His compromise is different to the ones being made by black ex-players, as it is based upon how the system changes when other white men, whom he has not previously worked with, come into more senior position to his, without any recognition for the need for a white mask. His mask is dependent on how he is accepted by these men; race is deemed irrelevant.

Wallace introduces the possibility that white men are made vulnerable by other white men, but when he compares the opportunities for black ex-players to move into these industries he shows that they are subjected to totally different cultural and political pressures inside and outside the football context:

I think the opportunities for black players are less than for white coaches; it's just a fact of life throughout English society. I think somebody needs to break in on that side; it needs a high profile black player. In my time in football colour doesn't really come into it, I haven't seen much on the surface, whether it's underlined in Chairmen or Directors I don't know. (Wallace Brent)

Wallace sees that, despite the lack of opportunities for black players, coaching is a system he can get into without representing his race. Both inside football and in English society he shares this luxury. He reinforces the fact that there are different rules and expectations that are often implicit for black and white men trying to get into the system.

The contradiction in Wallace's life is that he walked out of his job after a better opportunity was offered at a high profile club. He had dismissed the rules that he had adhered to. He had learnt a crucial lesson as a white man: that his career needs were more important than any loyalty to a club. He left behind a set of partners with whom he had worked closely during the previous few years. Although Wallace reveals that white men do not always relate to other white men through friendships, there still is a process of familiarity that is not shared by the black ex-players. They are able to operate within the norm of whiteness as the invisible centre that defines the professional culture itself. The race cognizance of the black ex-players stands in stark contrast to cognizance of white ex-players where through their second narratives the racism that is unsaid and almost apparent in this system is made concrete and visible.

The Changing Narratives of the Black Players: Outsiders and the Increasingly Disappointed

The second narratives of the black ex-players show an increasing awareness of a system that functions through the unconscious formation of white male nepotism, which is self-policing, and that limits their life chances as black men in this industry. Darren Smith, in his second interview, demonstrated that he had become more disillusioned with the system, as he began to feel that there were rules operating within this system that act without any level of accountability:

> I have never applied for a coaching job anywhere, I have never seen them come up and they don't put an advert in the Sun you know. I don't know why I haven't made it, the only other thing I can do is to write to the 92 League Clubs and say that Darren Smith is available. But then somebody in the game will say, oh, have you done it, but how many people have got jobs, have done it. (Darren Smith)

Darren sees a system that does not work, formally, equitably or on a multiracial basis. He is slowed down by a process and procedure that nobody else complies with, searching for a job without any personal contact. The harder he tries to work to be included into the system, the greater is the social distance and the more invisible are the routes that his white male counterparts are using. He sees an institution that preaches meritocracy, but practises inequality resolutely, by design and by implication. This sense of not knowing or seeing the closed doors or how the system works is compounded by Darren seeing the types of black players that white men feel comfortable working with. He then rationalizes that success is purely dependent on having the right kinds of relationships with white men that might require him to compromise himself as a black man who does not want to be subservient:

> You know Andrew passes, good luck to him, but I am sure people were saying to him, don't be seen with those black lads. Because we be at lunch and it be funny how some white lads would come straight over to the table without thinking about it and you see others looking. They would drop their shoulders and say that table looks too black, and you see arseholes like Andrew doing the same thing. (Darren Smith)

Darren's comment shows he's mystified as to how these processes of acceptance operate or how he should act and with whom he should associate to progress. For Darren, his inability to see how to play the 'white man's' game leads him to think that he represents a form of black masculinity, a defiance that the system cannot accommodate. He then internalizes his personal failure, as opposed to seeing how the system cannot deal with difference and diversity. This leads to a self-alienation as he realizes that he cannot take the level of exploitation needed to stay in the system.

Darren now sees more clearly a form of white male nepotism, where he cannot become part of the football family. To survive he must become detached from a system in which he has no chance to establish himself. It is from this position of detachment that Darren understands that the system will include him on a lower level than his white counterpart, for less money, and that he will have to work harder to make less progress. His response is to work hard to be included into one role whilst he experiences exclusion when trying to move into a higher position. He sees a system that will only accept and recognize him in a less powerful position as a black man if he wants to keep his autonomy. Darren continues to stay outside the system, losing two jobs as an academy coach with a series of clashes with white men who give his job to their friends. He moves completely out of this system and runs a series of local Sunday teams, a situation in which he knows he can more effectively control both the setting and how he works with it.

This tension of autonomy and acceptance in getting an English coaching qualification and wanting the same privileges as white English colleagues is articulated by David Boyce. Boyce becomes sceptical about the value of a coaching qualification as a route to a job in his second interview, where he highlights his return to a world where competition is no longer based upon a level playing field:

> The job is going to come through another channel, somebody you know, or somebody you know has got a job and they want to take you with them. But there are a few players in the game I have played with, there's Kerry Francis, he's not really got a management post, there's Tony Kay, but I don't know him that well. I like to try my hand outside of Football; I won't get a job on the strength of this coaching badge, not in England. (David Boyce)

David sees that he needs to have a close relationship with somebody in the system to succeed; a coaching qualification is worthless compared with being familiar with the right kind of white men. He sees that these forms of familiarity with white men are based upon being part of a distinct English culture, getting close up and inside these race associations through the mundane processes of talking and eating to form the necessary bonds from his playing days. He has to decide if it is worth making transparent the types of racism invested in the rules that exclude black men who are English or to forge the performance conducive for white men to feel safe about his entry.

Reluctant to change to meet the values of the white players, he saw that he would only be given a chance if he could make the way that racism operates insignificant, or he would have to move from a career in the system to a safer option outside of the profession. He thus retired from the professional game to return to his first love music, and then took a job with a semi-professional game, but as yet he has not returned to the professional context as a coach. He did not expect to become a coach, so he does not feel he has failed by being unrealistic about a very exclusive system.

The next two black players show how their relationships with white men inside the system shapes their understanding of how offside racism operates through the power that white men have over them.

Manipulation of White Male Networks and Nepotism

This theme of the control white men have over black ex-players in their move into the system is reflected more specifically in the second interview with Ian Harris, who began to see his life as having to negotiate and bid for a position alongside them. Ian had completed his UEFA A coaching badge, Bristol City had been promoted from the second to the first division and Ian's relationship with John Bless, his first team manager, led to more delegated responsibilities. He thus began to access the closed doors through his contact with a white chairman and a white board of directors from which he was once excluded. This contact and responsibility creates an illusion of being included, of actually progressing through the system: 'I don't really want the hazards of management. If I wanted to be a boss right now I would find this difficult, I don't think I have the experience. My goals are to keep learning to acquire the knowledge, to manage the club' (Ian Harris).

Ian still thinks that he has to progress in stages despite his new association with white men. He defers to them by alienating himself to a space outside of management through a sense of inferiority. He is only worthy in the eyes of white men if he knows all facets of the job, before he can progress. His tactic of almost sticking to his white manager works successfully as he moves with him from one job into another and eventually in the setting of the premiership. But again his position remains the same. He ironically experiences what white men try to achieve: he becomes rooted. The disadvantage is that he becomes a fixture and is locked to one position for the rest of his life. He experiences uncertainties and self-questioning that were not evident in my white sample, because he begins to accept this is as far as he can go.

This struggle to be 'worthy' in the eyes of white men was also reflected in Stephen Bridges' second narrative. During this period he continues to seek acceptance into a permanent position as a coach, when he is promoted to being the first team coach, as he begins to understand the ambivalent and implicit forms of white male behaviour, as he also gets closer to the old, white establishment:

> You must remember I am a coach not a manager and in my experiences in sitting in the director's box I haven't felt any inward or outward signs of racism. But I am in a different position I am a first team coach, where I am there watching the game with other coaches. In terms of the board I think it's the old establishment, and they are harder to breakdown. (Stephen Bridges)

From Stephen's position in the director's box he has to assess the unpredictable outcomes that surround being around white chairmen when he has little exposure to their values and perceptions. He must read the ways these white men operate and the implications of their unconscious racist acts, particularly the perception of his capability to do the job. Thus he was left in a vulnerable position as he was relegated to being the reserve team coach without knowing how this decision was taken. When Stephen's first team manager was sacked he was replaced by another white manager, who brought in his white male assistant to take over Stephen's role as the first team coach. Here racism operated on a 'behind the scenes', implicit level, because Stephen was absent from the negotiation, he was absent from the histories involved in these personnel working together to establish their place in this system.

Stephen faces moments where he does not know how the rules governing his ability to move through the system operate. He cannot flag up these offside forms of racism that take place through the way white men select other white men with limited consideration of their skill and competence. Stephen's situation is similar to Ian's. Their identities become fixed, like the school keeper who is always in the same position whoever the headmaster is. The success of his story is that he obtained a part-time position as number two to an international team coach, mirroring exactly the same status he had at both the local and international levels.

Inverting Forms of Whiteness and 'Being Ahead of the Game'

Les Turner, in his second interview, began to see the problems black ex-players face in being accepted into the system after his first response was to work hard and to forget about how he was being judged as a black man. He sees race as an important issue that emerges at a significant point in his life and in this relationship between sport and society:

> I don't care what you say it's difficult no matter what your colour is. But I think racism in society is more noticeable, in soccer it's subtler. In terms of me making cultural changes, I don't think I do consciously, sometimes you may change and your may not. But you do feel under pressure as a black coach, you can't put your finger on it. There are few of you; yeah I feel I can't afford to fail. (Les Turner)

Les began to see the implications for his survival when his colour was called to question in relation to his ability to do the job. He saw that he was engaged in a system where it was improbable that he would be able to do his job without being accountable for being black. His colour-blind strategy was dented by realizing that, as one of a small group of black people, his survival and the progression of other black personnel were dependent upon him doing well. Unlike the white ex-players, Les performance shapes whether the system can accommodate other black ex-players.

When sacked from his job at Mansfield, he moved out of the Football League to manage a non-League club, as the implicit forms of racism that were initially obscured in his first interview became explicit. This led Les to see a second system where black coaches are only given one chance, facilitating a political reorientation to challenge the power white men have:

> I think a lot of them need to make more noises about why they are not being accepted. It's very tricky because if black ex-players start saying they want to be managers, people in authority don't won't them in positions because they think they will cause trouble. Unfortunately whether you like it or not we have a persona where we are looked upon as dishonest, they always think I better watch out, but they might not say it. (Les Turner)

Les's narrative shows how one's experience can change one's cognizance of racism. The experience of being sacked reveals a system where he sees how white men are threatened by black men, how through their negative stereotypes they use their power to exclude black men. For Les there is a need to contest these stereotypes of black people being dishonest to get to the core of how white men use their authority to preserve their position. During this period Les moved out of the Football League and back in again and has become one the leading role models, also playing an active role in exposing the process of racism. Unlike many of the players in this sample he makes and establishes very clear links between how racism operates in society and how it filters through and influences his life in this system.

This idea of challenging the perceptions of white men from the outside is further explored in the case of Tony Francis. Tony tries to invert these processes of race exclusion, by trying to pre-empt the way white men undermine black men by expecting them to follow their instructions.

Tony had been given the first team coaching job at Exeter on a temporary basis. He recognized that with the departure of his manager he would be under less pressure to work in his ways and less dependent on this white man to validate his competence. He was, however, continually hindered by having to deal with the ongoing question that white men do not face: whether or not he was given the job because he is black:

> I have got this job and I can prove that I can do this job; they know I can do this job. I have been here for four and half years. I haven't got the job because I am black. I have the ultimate respect of all the players. I hope as time goes by I have the respect as the first team coach, but they know me, but one of the things I am, is very honest I tell them that. In terms of being one of the few black managers at the moment I haven't really thought about it yet. (Tony French)

Tony's survival in this system depends on his determination to dispel the demons of black men having to prove to the people around them that they can manage in a white environment. His cognizance changed from having to develop the right performance to convince white men of his ability, to a cognizance that linked to an inner belief that he could do the job. This relationship, between one's belief and one's performance was tested by the new processes and the new personnel Tony confronted, detecting a different form of racism in the structures of English soccer in a system where he would need to be more pre-emptive around the white men at this level of the organization: 'I am well schooled in the English culture; I am schooled in their way of thinking. They say one thing but I am always ahead of them, I know what they are thinking before they are thinking it. You got to be ahead of the Directors you have to be planning ahead' (Tony French).

Tony's progress in this system is dependent upon studying the idiosyncrasies of white men, so that he can deal with these moments of racism re-coded in the different ways white men work, think and behave. In terms of football metaphors this strategy by Tony represents an 'interception' because he now reads the situations that he may experience before they happen. He moves from a strategy of compromise to a position of empowering himself in the system where he attempts to disrupt the racist misconstructions made of his role as a black man. These misconstructions had a powerful effect after he lost his job as the senior coach and then returned again to his previous post as the reserve coach. He was back where he started, which was more preferable than actually going out of the system altogether. His narrative indicates that he is continually adjusting his approaches to white men just to get a job, a position to save being rejected, an approach similar to Darren's.

This ability to intercept, to invert the power of individual white men was not possible for William Marke in the context of the Football Association, a totally different environment from a football club because it is not based on a system of number one's and number two's but instead involves having control of a region or a national team. William suggests, that, in his new relationships in this setting, the task of 'intercepting' and inverting the power of white men is denied because of the of the low regard for him as a black coach in a very institutional hierchiacal setting. William develops a more guarded approach to his life in this system when he asked to take an English team to a tournament in Nigeria as their under-19s coach:

Nobody wanted to take the team out there, they thought as white men they would be in danger and I know they can't stand what they think would be extremely poor conditions, maybe they thought it be easier for a black man to accept those things. In any situation there are games that you have to play, so you have to be sensible. I don't think people blatantly come out and be racist to you in institutions do they, people articulate things in different ways, so if there is racism it needs to be swept under the cover. (William Marke)

William articulates a disguised form of racism through the very little respect given to him as a black man, sent to Africa where it is assumed that he is instinctively more qualified and naturally 'at home'. He faces a paradox in that this degrading form of racism can be disguised by celebrating Tony's role as representing an important advance in the emergence of black coaches, despite the scoring of an anti-racism own goal. William learns that he has to play this game to advance his career in an industry where he is undermined by being 'shut away', so to cope William depersonalizes his relationship with the white men he works under, his managers, the directors and the members of the Football Council. He resigns himself to the fact that he cannot influence their racist mentality, nor can he effect individual and institutional changes in the system because of his marginalized position as a black man:

> As I get older and the more I work in this place it just got to the point that I just look around and the stories, it is so inbred. I think it is very difficult to change things from the heart. Some of their attitudes the way they are, the way people think, the way they are towards black people, it's their attitude towards people. I am saying would they let you out with their daughters? No probably. But the same scaly geezer that is white, they probably would. (William Ramsey)

William's use of the metaphor of the 'white man's daughter' reveals how far white men in soccer are prepared to accept difference, to extend their nepotism to the black outsider, to let the black man go out with his daughter. It becomes impossible to detect their private racist thoughts and feelings they harbour about his role in the organization, even when he is working alongside them. William realizes that he is in a system where it is impossible to work out the different ways that individual white men operate or the collective and shared ways they make the system work. Consequently William totally moves out of the English game to a new country, not because of a lack of aspiration or competence, but because of a lack of aspiration and a competence within the system to accept and embrace black ex-players.

Throughout this year of interviews I realized, when talking to the seven black ex-players about these experiences, there was a risk of overidentifying and wanting to protect them more assertively, rather than showing the contradictory ways they were either being included or excluded. On an interpersonal level it was easier to develop an affinity with the black ex-players as black men, who had similar family, school, political and cultural experiences to my own, and similar experiences of discrimination and exclusion from the external world of soccer. It was also more painful to see and hear the discrimination they experienced as part of the practice of being in this system, and the way race was seen as their problem and part of their paranoia. One player from Birmingham acknowledged a form of transference taking place in relating to me as his younger brother, which enabled him to be very radical in his assessment of the racism he had experienced in the game and during one of our interviews in his front room he said:

> You know these white people, those white, middle class people in high positions, who still think we are slaves will never give us a job. There is a fear of black men in foot-ball, not in the playing, when you are all in it together, but when you're going for their job unless you happen to be one of those uptown blacks. (Darren Smith)

He then went very silent, expressing a fear about how the tape would be used and I assured him that it would not be used publicly without his permission. But in this one comment I realized how I represented the fear of the power white men hold in terms of his future in the game, even when it was not my intention to be a spy. The interviews thus became a way to understand his reluctance to challenge racism, to be complicit and non-confrontational and, to 'play the white man', as only the 'uptown black' can do.

–4–

The Public and Private Lives
of Black Managers

In other words the black man should no longer be confronted by the dilemma turn white or disappear, but he should be able to take cognizance of a possibility of existence. In other words if society makes difficulty for him because of his colour, if in his dreams I establish the expressions of an unconscious desire to change colour, my object will not be of that of dissuading him from it by advising him to 'to keep his place' on the contrary, my consciousness will be to push him into a position to chose action. (Fanon, 1967: 100)

The above quotation from Fanon (1967) is a useful way to explore how black players who become managers deal with their public and their private lives when confronting the pressures to be white in the institutions of football management. Fanon's (1967) idea of the 'white mask' reveals its potential, I suggest, to become an internal mechanism to operate inside the professional cultures of football, to develop a variety of responses to the unconscious acts of white men. The 'white mask' thus represents a subjective strategy to interpret black managers' experiences – a strategy that is flexible enough to mirror the idiosyncratic behaviour of white men. It enables black men to manage their feelings about racism inside the institutions of management and to change and adjust their identities as black men. For black women in the management role, it helps analyse the need for a 'white masculine mask' in dealing with the fear of walking into a white male organization and making visible forms of masculinity that black men take for granted as shared across the colour line.

These forms of shared masculinity can be analysed through the experiences of the early black ex-players who failed to make the transition into management, where the 'white mask' has an important function in mirroring the lack of faith white men have in them to perform in the institutional world of management. By comparing these experiences to the biographies of recent black ex-players who have become managers in the English game the theme of being owned or controlled by white men can be analysed by Malcolm X's (1965) notion of the 'house nigger'. The 'house nigger' as discussed in Chapter 1, becomes an important metaphor to explore how black ex-players' entry into management operates within the constraints of white personnel. Malcolm X's (1965) quotation below illustrates the historical pressures black men faced to respond to the order of the white man, to become his 'puppet':

> Well, slavery times 'house' and 'yard' Negroes had become more sophisticated, that was all. When now the white man picked up the telephone and dialled his 'house' and 'yard' Negroes, why, he didn't even need to instruct the trained black puppets. (Malcolm X, 1965: 341).

I suggest that black managers see similar types of racism as those that made them comply with white men 400 years ago, but in more complicated ways. This leads to an number of industries, including football, where white men are reluctant to see that they are denying black men the opportunities of being individuals. Consequently the historical influences of being in the white world of management leads to different formulas for black managers to make sense of their place in an institution where they want to be more that just black men, through the use of the 'white mask'.

Donning an Onside 'White Mask' in Management

The 'white mask' was used in the work of Fanon (1967) to describe the pressures placed on black men in post-colonialist society to adopt the white man's language and culture in order to be accepted. The implication for Fanon (1967), as suggested in the quotation below, was that the black man had to act like a white man to gain status. They had to enact a public performance through the 'white mask' beyond the black skin in the white worlds of European society: 'The black man has two dimensions, one with his fellows, and the other with the white man. A Negro behaviour differs with a white man and with another Negro. This self division is a direct result of colonial subjugation (Fanon, 1967: 40).

As black ex-players progress from their playing careers to a coaching qualification to seeking a job as a coach or a manager the traditional use of the 'white mask' changes its function. Race is not as fixed as Fanon (1967) assumes. This is because forms of racism now operate in the competition between men within a shared code of silence in a profession with few cross-cultural exchanges, where you do not flag up racism if you want to be considered for a management job. The 'white mask' then reveals the compulsion to be mute to conceal these power inequalities with white men, if black men are to stand any chance of being selected.

This propensity to disguise white men's racism can be highlighted by the forms of exclusions black men confronted in trying to become managers in the English game in the late 1990s, especially this perception of the industry needing a particularly type of black man as illustrated in this comment by Brendon Batson:

> I always said the acid test is would a black Bryan Robson have made it or a white John Barnes. At the top level there will be those with the financial clout, hopefully you will

see more and more players moving into these positions. I remember speaking to Cecil Burke when he thought of going into management and I said do everything, show that you have a good CV and if nothing happens you can show this is institutionalized. (Brendon Batson)

Brendon's comment reveals an industry that can only accommodate white men, so the need to act like the white man represents an implicit form of racism, as it defines acceptability and competence in relation to the silent criterion of race. Conversely black players now have to transcend the biological images made of them in the playing field, to reshape the mind set and the stereotypes attached to their body, to match the cultural needs of the institutions of management. So the question of whether a black Bryan Robson would have got a management position, disguises the fact that black ex-players may have to act like Bryan Robson to demonstrate that they are at ease in working with white men in this system.

It is important to say that not all black players will agree on the best strategy to get a management job. As noted in the first chapter, black players are not all the same and will see and experience the institution of management like the entry to the playing field, as dependent on how they conceptualize the importance of racism. Whilst there has been an overt focus to report racism in the stadium as a distraction to revealing the institutional barriers faced in management, the voices of black ex-players trying to make the transition have been marginalized. The management role involves greater economic and political influence. It is a world much closer to the world of white directors and commercial business personnel, to the closed doors and invisible spaces that black men in and outside the world of sport have been excluded from. How these closed doors operate and the actions necessary to enter can be best understood in the rare moments when black ex-players take the risk of talking openly about how they perceive and understand the possibility of finding the key to get in.

On one occasion at a launch I was fortunate to interview two black ex-players with contrasting views on the work and efforts needed to get a job as a manager inside English football:

It's hard, man, it's politics and at the end of the day its about big business, so how are they going to let a brother deal with the pure string of a club that could be 20 million or 15 million pounds, they are not going to give you that squeeze. Look at the brother at Middlesborough, Anderson, he had a chance to break down barriers at Barnsley, but he jumped ship, to be second in command elsewhere, because he knew if he got sacked tomorrow he would get a job somewhere else. He worked with Bryan Robson and said I might as well stay here, stay on the gravy trail instead of looking at doing things on my own . . . He bottled it because he knew at the end of the day it wasn't going to happen. (Andy Frail)

Andy in this comment, shows the frustration of not being trusted with white men's money. It's a view that resonated from wider society, and relates to how much according to Malcolm X (1965) black players moving into management are puppets with no real economic power.

This theme of the puppet is contested further in his reference to Viv Anderson's failure to assert his position as a manager in his own right, but taking the safer option of become reliant on another white man who will take him along where he goes, so safeguarding his passport to a job in an industry where it was made precarious because he was one of few black men around. What Andy suggests on one level is a lack of confidence to expose oneself to a management system where racism is implicit. It does not openly claim that it prefers black players in the subordinate role. The classical test of this theory was the black management team of Ricky Hill and Chris Ramsey in 2001, who were sacked after three months, and replaced by two white men. Their experience set a precedent that that black managers may need to be realistic about their movement into management and the role they are going to be offered in English football as reflected in this second comment from Andy:

> If you got people like Wrighty saying he doesn't want to be a manager, who else is there? There's Ince and there's Barnes. I am too militant for those guys, my reputation is that I tell it as it is. That's not how they want it to be, it's all mate. How can a taxi driver and a butcher become a chief scout at a club? They talk about racism through the years but hey don't talk about management. (Andy Frail)

In Andy's second comment we begin to see the unfortunate but also depressing implications of black managers setting their stall too high and failing. A message is given that they must start from the bottom, especially if they are perceived as too radical. This position of being too militant is not simply based on speaking out, but not accepting convention, especially in the context when white men with no comparable experiences of playing, accelerate from outside the football world and get jobs ahead of them.

At this moment, whilst talking to Andy, Brendon Batson appeared, also from a completely different era, the 1970s and 1980s, and a completely different position: he was then Deputy Chief Executive of the Professional Footballers Association. A conversation began between the two ex-players, Andy from the period of the 1990s and outside of the system as he retired recently. Both articulated the point from the first chapter that the perspective of black men in football will not be the same:

> Do everything, get your coaching qualification and when you present yourselves, you are actually the same, so if a job comes up, so you apply and they filter through the applications and they say has he got that. So when some body presents themselves and

I can say they have got fifty caps for England and they have played at the top flight. John Barnes has he put his hat in the ring, Wrighty says he's interested in youth football, he has dropped himself out. (Brendon Batson)

Brendon advocates the belief that black ex-players should do everything they can to get into management, to do exactly what the system requires of them based upon an assumption that it may work, that people like Wright and Barnes, because of their high-profile positions, can transcend race barriers. The central problem with Brendon's position inside the system is that he poses the official version, which is not adopted and embraced by the manipulative strategies used by white men. I don't suggest that Brendon has become the white man's 'puppet', or he is simply a 'house nigger' controlled by white men in this management world, but he has to consider the cost of speaking out and challenging a system that pays his wages, that supports his identity and may depend on him being the only one due to the fear of large numbers of new black managers threatening white men in their positions as argued in Andy's response:

But that's wrong saying that, you know and I know managers are washed up and they have had million of chances, they are the same people who throw their hands in for everyone job. There's Wrighty saying he wants to be youth team manager, that's not positive. (Andy Frail)

Andy's response may again be articulated from his position outside of the game, but it is a position in which he can be more open and honest about the completely different methods used by white men. He articulates frustration that, irrespective of their past and their experiences, or whether they are washed up, white men stick around, on this restricted merry go around, constantly open to offers. This point of whether Ian Wright simply prefers another merry go around, which is a much smaller circus, and well below the ones being used by white managers is a crucial issue. The issue that needs to be examined is whether Wright is internalizing his inferiority, or making a choice simply in relation to his own career, which Andy and Brendon perceive and respond to in completely different ways:

No that's not his choice at the end of the day he doesn't know how powerful he is. (Andy Frail)

All I am saying is that those players in positions, would a black Souness or a black Wilkins have got a job? Until we have these players of equal status, when they present themselves and they say they want to go into management if they don't get in you can say it's because they don't get the same equal opportunities as their white counterparts, until that time we have not really got anybody, John Barnes would be one of those ones. There is a certain type of person that suits management, like a Bryan Robson, good in front of the camera, who handles themselves. I think there is a certain profile that you got to present, and that profile runs across both black and white men. (Brendon Batson)

The contrast between the responses is interesting because of the ways black managers are seen as getting or not getting into this industry. Firstly, Andy suggests black players undermine their power, whilst Brendon advocates that they do have power because if they are high profile, then they should have the same respect as high-profile white players, but they do not test their power by putting themselves forward. The major problems with Brendon's position are the huge psychological and institutional pressures black ex-players have to confront to test whether racism operates in the movement into management. The journey for a player seeking a place as a manager is both daunting by its newness and dependent upon totally different rules that the system does recognize, especially when the issue of colour is called into question when the higher establishment decide who should be the best candidate for the job. The following dialogue between these two black players reveals the contradictory ways in which this system is perceived as operating in their lives and the lives of other black players:

Batson: But to the ones who can hire and fire the colour isn't an issue. I don't think we have a high profile who has presented themselves, who has says I want to be a manager with no qualifications and no experience. If you going to battle down doors, Wrighty is the person, if Wrighty stood up and said I want to be a manager they would listen. I think John Barnes is the one who has got that profile.

Frail: It's alright saying you want to be a manager, but you have got to be a manager to open doors.

Batson: Do you fancy you chances at management?

Frail: I am too coarse.

Batson: I know, but you would have go through the process of youth team manager, going through the traditional routes, but John Barnes because of his background, because of the way he handles himself.

Frail: But answer me this question. It's all about timing, when I look around I have been brought by all the England managers. They turn around and say Alan Smith is a good manager, he's not a good coach. Ray Lewington what has he done in the game to say he is a good coach? I can't understand how these guys keep getting jobs and they haven't done anything.

Batson: It's a treadmill, and you know Andy it's about arselicking.

Frail: It's about politics.

Batson: Yeah you have got to do this, but if you do get that chance, I told Cryrille go and get your coaching badge, cause in the game everybody got to have a licence. If you can't get in that way, try another way, keep your head down. That's what he's doing at West Brom, he's got in there, there has been a change

of management, but he's not in the firing line if a new manager comes in. as he's reserve team boss. So do you fancy you chance as a manager.
Frail: No, it's all the shit I have experienced.

These comments reveal in one conversation the complexity of the issues facing the emergence of black managers during this period of time. Firstly, Brendon repeats the theme that we cannot know or see racism unless black players come forward, especially if they are on the same level as other white ex-players who come in with no qualifications or relevant past. Brendon actually moves his position by suggesting that the need to 'battle the door' if the first strategy, working through the system, does not work. He promotes Wright and Barnes as the martyrs and activists who seem to show that it is possible to have a black manager, but it is up to them to come forward as the system will not promote them. It is a perspective shared by Frail but in a much more assertive way, in that Barnes and Wrighty carry the whole responsibility of the first and new generation of black managers. Their introduction and success make it permissible for the system to open its doors for black managers to be given a chance, not in terms of their competence, but as black managers. Both Brendon and Frail, through their conversation, are creating a class structure amongst black players, which is similar to the processes that take place in football management. High-profile players start at the top, the rest have to work through the system from the bottom upwards. This is reflected when Brendon suggests that Frail's career in management is dependent on starting at the youth team level, whilst Barnes can start right at the top. The significant difference, as Frail recognizes, is that Barnes is seen as the acceptable face of whiteness, more likely to be accepted as a puppet, whilst he, Frail, is perceived as too rough. Both polarize the political acceptance of black players, based on these qualities of compliance and defiance. They situate them as Malcolm X refers to, the house and the nigger. So John Barnes becomes the white man's puppet, the 'house nigger', and Frail then positions himself as the 'field nigger', angry and unable to be accepted into the white man's house. At this point a consensus emerges and they get to the very centre of the informal issues of management, the quasi political issues, and at this moment Brendon presents a radical change by admitting that it is about 'arselicking'. It is what Malcolm X (1965) refers to as the house nigger personified in the black players doing all they can do despite the emotional cost, to be accepted as a manager in the English game. This is a deferential perspective, which is further reinforced by this next black player who has been attempting to get into the management chair:

Of course at the end of the day it's all about power. From my point of view, white Caucasian men, there's a fear factor there. You never know boardrooms hidden agendas. Those white guys from million pound backgrounds, do they understand having a black guy as their manager? They want a bigger profile than ordinary white guys. Some black guys can do it, they can transcend race. You look at Ruud Gullit, you look at John Barnes. It's the ordinary guy that has got the qualifications, who have good enthusiasm, will they get the chance? (Cecil Burke)

In Cecil Burke's story he returns to the rigid need to meet these white male expectations, which involve keeping happy white boardroom members who may only take a risk with high-profile black players as the only people who can transcend race. Cecil realizes that he does not have the power to change their fixed ideas of race, these fears of white men that operate within the closed doors of the boardroom. He realizes that white men use their power to force black men to act on their terms if they want a job as a manager in this profession, creating a situation similar to the pressures placed on black men in the playing field. For Cecil, he's helpless, he does not see how white men construct their beliefs about him as a black man, so he does not know how he can still resist the pressure to be the white man's servant, to condemn himself as the 'house nigger'. Beneath his mask Cecil reconciles himself to the fact that it is impossible to transcend the one-dimensional stereotypes made by white men, who are inflexible and fail to acknowledge him as an individual in his own right. The ongoing challenge to black managers is to resist internalizing their role as the 'house nigger' and to free themselves psychologically from needing permission from white men to manage in their own right. As black ex-players move from the playing field they have to face the cold reality that the brotherhood that went across the colour line is broken, white men no longer see them as team members, but they become part of a competitive job market that is institutionally different from the competition in trying to get into the first team

The processes by which white men block the arrival of black players moving into management is reflected in Michael Andrews' comment about trying to get a job as a manager in the English game:

I made a lot of applications. They look at you and you're black and then all the stereotypes come out and they joke, but that's what they see. You have got the problem to overstep all of that and show them that you can do the job and that's why you need to be successful at the very top. They don't know the black person, but all it takes is oh yeah, it doesn't seem to be a good idea. If you look at all the current managers, who have had problems with drink, but that has never prevented them from getting another job. (Michael Andrews)

In Michael's comment there is a realization that no matter how he performs through the 'white mask' he will never be accepted, he can never dispel the stereotypes that affect his progress. The mask becomes redundant as a tool to present to white men, showing them that black men can act white. Thus it is impossible to become the 'house nigger', to be a servant to the white man, because all the opportunities that arise in this setting are automatically given to white men. Consequently, although black players may try to assume the culture of white men in their effort to become managers, in their internal world they recognize they may have to 'sell out' without being able to change the rules that govern their exclusion. He has to operate in an industry where acceptance is then based on something more than performing the public image of the 'house nigger'.

This need for a new performance and a new internal reckoning can be analysed through the ways that recent black managers have adapted to the management setting. Unfortunately there has been little analysis of the complicated ways that individual black managers faced the discreet forms of racism in the management of industries especially in relation to the issues of masculinity. Pat Link more specifically articulates the complex relationships between the 'white mask' and masculinity as a black woman, by describing how the forms of male domination filter from the world outside football into the context of football management:

> I think somebody needs to break through and probably act as a voice or a spokesperson. It can be done and you should not be intimidated by the whole set up. Cause I believe it is scary, its scary to put yourself out there unknown in a white world, in an all white situation, its scary because colour always becomes an issue. (Pat Link)

As a black woman she makes more acutely transparent the power of white men to create anxiety and uncertainty when being around them at this level of the organization.

The Private Worlds of Black Managers

It is by exploring the inner worlds of past black managers (Viv Anderson of Barnsley and Middlesborough, Chris Kamara, ex-manager of both Bradford City and Stoke City, Ricky Hill and Chris Ramsey of Luton Town, Rudd Gullit of Chelsea) that the accusation of being 'coconuts' (black on the outside, white on the inside) opens up how they were unfairly judged inside and outside the football industry. Unfortunately black managers who do not talk about their relationships with white men are automatically seen as colluding with racism in this setting because of their silence. They face a polarized pressure of having to be black or white, vulnerable to the terms that become fixed in measuring their ability to fit into the cultures of management, no matter what their cultural background or the complexity of their racial identity. To survive within these fixed terms Ruud Gullit (1997) describes himself as an 'overseas coach', so he is able to escape the traps faced by black managers born in England, having to separate their identities as black men in an English management system. This enables Gullit (1997) to operate with a multicultural identity in both his private and public worlds, so he liberates himself to move around the system despite whether others may feel he is playing a very complex 'race game'.

The challenge for black men who were either born in England or who have lived most of their lives in England, and who become managers, is to begin to understand their role, both politically and professionally. It is to come to terms with a system that is continually judging black men both historically and in the context of the perceptions that exist about them outside of football. In my first interview with John Barnes, he faced the task of understanding how he was positioned in an industry where the tensions between black and white men are not acknowledged. This, I believe, is because black men become so absorbed with issues of dealing with racism as a professional practice that the task of talking about their failure as men becomes too painful. This failure to enable black men to talk as individuals is rooted in the portrayal of John Barnes as the one high-profile black man who was expected to break into a predominantly white male profession. As an advert for the erosion of racism, he represents the collective voice of black players.

In the summer of 1998, John Barnes was offered the job of first team coach at Celtic Football Club, it was commented that he did not have the experience, he was not qualified and he did not understand the traditions of the community of Celtic supporters. These perceptions tested his capacity to work within the traditions of white men who have gone before him even before he started. I interviewed John whilst he was first team coach at Celtic after a number of phone calls to Newcastle and Charlton where John had played. I was contacted by his secretary on a Thursday and was told John would be prepared to offer me an interview on the following Monday. That weekend Celtic lost to Hearts at home, 3–2, after taking a two nil lead. There were rumours of players' dissent and the board were unhappy with John's overall performance. During our interview John talked earnestly about his desire to move into management from the age of thirty-two and his feelings about how he saw white men influencing his transition:

> You're talking about it being a white man's world and it is and we know that, so maybe there's a fear of us. There are people's perceptions because there are few black managers. People say if you fail is that an indictment on black people, are they saying if I don't succeed black managers can't manage? That is the most racist question I have ever been asked. What about white managers who fail, does that mean white people can't manage. (John Barnes)

John's comment is an attempt to make the 'white mask' redundant so he can remove the conditions upon which white men judge him and the pressure of having to be always representing his race, to be accountable in ways white men are not. He understands at this level of the organization that he has to operate in and amongst white men who control the industry, but he does not want to be the victim of failure for his whole community. In trying to separate out and protect his private identity from how he is constructed on a public level, John sees the dangers in being measured by stereotypes that have nothing to do with his ability to do his job as a manager:

> People often ask me if I am British, Jamaican or what. That's not who I am, it's not part of my profession. I am a professional player, who is a manager called John Barnes. Professionally I am English, working within a Scottish club to which I am fully committed. Who I am is when you take me away from this environment, to my family, that's who I am, when I am with my friends, the conversations I have, the thoughts I have away from my job. This is what I am, a football manager. (John Barnes)

John seeks the same privileges as white managers who are not judged in relation to their racial and national identities by his intent to maintain a distinction between his private and public world. He simply wants to be John Barnes the manager. He finds he is always associated with myths and fantasies he has no control over, which contribute towards an illusion that may have nothing to do with who he is. His ongoing struggle is to remove the mystery of how he is seen in relation to whether he can manage a Scottish football club because he may not be sure if he is Jamaican first or English first. John wants to hold on to his private world and prevent it intervening into his life as an employee. He faces having to deal with the reservations of white men who question his professional loyalties and his ability to represent and perpetuate the traditions of an industry that is built on historical white male patterns. The test for John, in trying to operate as an individual who is a black man, is to deal with a football world that wants to fix his identity. This need to categorize him leads John to see a form of racism that operates through white men's misconceptions. John is a black manager, his blackness comes first if he fails, or he's manager first if he succeeds. His strategy not to challenge these misconstructions reflects his inability to educate white men, to make their specific form of racism open, which may have detrimental implications for his survival. He sees that he has no influence over the ways that white men in the industry behave. It is impossible to mirror back the implications of them as only wanting to change on their terms and at their pace:

> When it came to the end of slavery, you know what got rid of slavery? When white people thought it was wrong for slavery, not when black people thought it was wrong for slavery. But as soon as white people started saying slavery is wrong we will abolish slavery. They won't change, what you have to do is let them hit you in the face. Eventually they say this is wrong and they will change. (John Barnes).

John's perception of change as passive and non-interventionist should not be read as selling out in his comparison to slavery, but part of his internal conversation in which he reasons with this dogmatic white world of management. He clearly assesses what change is possible amongst white men. His philosophy, that the transition of black players into management will be dependent upon white men, acting on the basis of moral guilt as in the slave period, mirrors the denial of white men to see the historical and repeating patterns of racism in their lives.

These patterns of white male power were made more apparent when John applied for several management jobs in England, believing that the outcome was dependent on fate as part of the idiosyncrasies of white male behaviour. The consequence was that John sees no clear logic in relation to his entry, he believes that there is no way of predicting how white men will operate when selecting black managers. He has to accept without being able to detect that racism may be an element within the selection process, because challenge may lead to white men becoming entrenched, making it more difficult for him to be trusted. John has to continually gear himself up to be accepted or rejected like any other manager, whilst knowing that white men covertly may not allow him the privilege of anonymity that comes with being a white manager. He operates between worlds. The professional world is similar to that of any other manager: in the office by 9.30 am, coaching until mid-day, afternoon meetings and occasional meetings with his board. In his other world he has to reconcile with the quality of his relationships with his line manager and the board that determines his existence:

> As the first team coach, you haven't got the long term, if you don't win something in the first year you are out. So my focus is just the first team, it's just the first team, Kenny's developing the club for the next twenty years. Kenny and the board are involved in buying first team players, I will target them in terms of coaching and the development of the team that is my responsibility. (John Barnes)

John's comment reveals his positioning to these white men and how he is precariously placed within this organization where he has little direct say over his life or in terms of how he's perceived. John has to analyse his performance as a manager in the context of being judged by standards that are developed by a new commercial business culture of white men. He's not familiar with their practices. Consequently when he was sacked after a range of poor results, he had to deal with trying to re-enter the industry. He felt he had been 'set up', having always seen this danger of being labelled as a black manager. By moving on to the experiences of Les Ball, I want to begin to compare the different strategies used by black ex-players to rationalize their lives as managers in a white institutional setting. Les shows the need for a flexible public response to white men as a black manager in an organization where he sees that he has to perform through and beyond the 'white mask' to be accepted. He was offered the joint care-manager's job at Bristol City. He has begun to manufacture a series of performances tuned in relation to how he has had to perform as a player during his career at Fulham, West Ham and at Bristol City. These performances are geared to the interface with white men he used to play with, who are now his employers:

If somebody tells a joke about black people I don't think that is racism, a joke is a joke, it's the way it is told, and there are certain people who put things in a certain way. But I think people treat me on my merits, I suppose if your aware of it you do feel the pressure, I see myself as a person and if people want to treat me in a certain way that is up to them. I see myself as a role model to other black lads, but that does not put pressure on me as one of few in the profession. (Les Ball)

Les's presentation to these personnel is influenced by assessing the cost of challenging acts of racism to assimilate into the expectations of white men in the world of management where he is on his own. His comment reveals the value of the 'white mask' as an internal conversation to explore how these microprocesses of being part of a team help him to evaluate what he is prepared to see and tolerate as racism. The analysis of the jokes told by white men is used to see how he is implicated in their world, so he can survive by making a distinction between racist comments and racist intent. Les can then position himself as a black manager who can also be unique and different, by virtue of showing he has the ability to be flexible in his response to the different acts of the white men he works with and what he needs to do to succeed as a manager irrespective of what they think of him:

I think we might have to work that much harder to succeed but that's life. People forget it isn't a black society, it's a Western society and I am from an African background and people do view you differently. It's harder as a manager and a coach, it's easier as a player because you just went out there and played, and people are not concerned about you as a person. As a manager you're got to be respected, you have got to adjust to so many individuals and thousand of different personalities. (Les Ball)

In this comment Les contextualizes the problems of being a black manager in a white Westernized society by identifying the ways football as an institution sees his blackness and not his individuality. His international perspective to his transition and role as a black ex-player who wants to be successful as a manager, leads to a formula: different responses to the perceptions and expectations of the white managers and directors who hire and fire. At the same time in his internal world, he can rationalize his feelings towards white men in this industry who construct him without sharing their repressed distortions. Through his internal reckoning Les can see that football is symbolic of Western society where white men may not want to change despite their individual personalities because their power is invested in their heritage. It is through these individual encounters with white men that a specific individualized 'white mask' is mastered in terms of managing the relationship between one's internal reckoning and one's performance, which contributes to the more complex processes of being a black manager.

For example Les was initially the first team manager at Gloucester City, he then became part of a three-man management team at Bristol City. When the first team manager left, the job was given to one of the two white men. Despite his disappointment, Les recognizes that he has to work within a culture where white men may unconsciously select another white man without being accountable in the same way as John Barnes is in relation to their race identity as white men. As a consequence Les has to be more diverse in his interactions with white men whilst also feeling confident in being accepted for who he is, irrespective of whether the people he works with want to patronize him or collude with their own vulnerability in always needing to be around other white men.

Les developed a mechanism, a form of inner conversation, whereby he can adjust his behaviour based upon the specific environment he is located in. This is a cognitive process, not recognized in black ex-players, in which they begin to mirror back in their internal world how they perceive white men behaving towards them. Using this process Les can decide on the type of performance that is needed to bridge the social distance between him and white men he may need to show he is capable of working with.

Les remained in this position before moving on to become a manager in his own right. He continues to face at the lower levels of the game this tension between when he is a manager and when he is a black manager and continues to use the mask as an internal reflection of how he is being perceived. In the case of Alex Walsh this process of black ex-players' inner reflections becomes a device that enables him to separate his identity as a manager from his identity as a black person.

This tension between being a manager and being a black manager results in an ongoing struggle in which black ex-players like Alex manage by dividing their worlds inside and outside the football management industry.

The background to the way Alex separates his worlds can be understood by noting that that his mother was from England and his father from Jamaica, but he was adopted and brought up by white English parents, so his social and political world is more diverse, but not necessarily its application. He played his early football in the lower leagues followed by a period at Crystal Palace, before moving on to Blackpool and his eventual club, Bury. Before his career as a manager Alex had been a player at Bury, then he was asked to take care of the reserve team on the day that his manager, Stan Bridges, left the job as first team manager. Alex then walked into the chairman's office and asked to take care of the team for the rest of the season. He was given the job. His appointment was made quietly, without the same level of public announcement given to the appointments of John Barnes. He did not have the same public scrutiny about his role as a black manager inside an English management system. As Alex talked about his work, getting into the job and his long-term ambitions, he revealed uneasiness about the task of confronting the pressures of being one of the few black men in a predominantly white profession:

I have been brought up in a white background but I know I am a black person. There has been no problem in that. I have been brought up in a white community but I have never known any racism towards me at all. But I think it goes on, its when you have a mixture of black and white people together. But I would like to go on and achieve much more and to set a precedent and encourage more black players to go into management. (Alex Walsh)

In his private thoughts Alex develops the ability to travel from his white community, his white heritage without feeling that he has lost his black identity, revealing the complexity of race as an identity inside football. As he moves from his white community into a football world, racism becomes a different type of problem. Racism becomes apparent in the interface between black and white people without any acknowledgment of the issues of power in this. This denial enables him to see that he still needs to carry out the day-to-day task of being a manager in an atmosphere where the conditions of racism are often discreet despite how he relates to or how he feels about the white men around him. He is not able to sensitize himself to the covert forms of racism taking place in management, which are different from the overt forms of racism that took place as a player:

I don't know why there are so few black managers in the game, it would be interesting to see how many are applying, but it shouldn't make any difference at all. It needs one of us to do well to achieve something and may be the petty minded people will take more notice, but I don't think it will make much difference. I have heard rumours in the game, but there are some managers who won't sign a black player, but I can't understand these people, but that's what I have heard and obviously it still goes on. (Alex Walsh)

Alex buys into the trap John Barnes tries to avoid. For black ex-players the transition into management depends on having to overachieve as black men, whilst knowing that this success may not change white men's perception.

In this next case example, Shaun Watson represents the type of black manager who does not consider racism to be a process that affects his potential to enter the structures of football and to be successful. He denies that processes of racism are at play both in his private world and in his public performance. He sees results as the most important criteria for acceptance.

Shaun's mother was from Canterbury, England, his father from Trinidad, but he had lived all his life in the north of England, which may suggest a regional aspect to his submissive approach to racism. During his career Shaun played for Charlton, Southend, Wolves and eventually Lincoln. He had been appointed manager at Lincoln after being promoted through the ranks from reserve team coach to first team coach.

His resistance to talking about the presence of racism in football enables him to live his life without feeling inhibited by something that is not real to him about the pressure as the only black manager in the premier league and the football league:

> I might have been the only black manager at the time, but it didn't really affect me. Managing a football team you are responsible for all the staff, 40 professionals. But the chairman sacked me, the chairman had a very large ego, he wanted to get involved in bits, which I resented. We had a few injuries and the lowest wage bill in the division, results hadn't gone well and the chairman decided to take over the management position. (Shaun Watson)

Despite Shaun experiencing the ultimate embarrassment of being displaced in his role as manager by the white chairman, he refutes the suggestion that white men can be racist so it's possible to keep the door open. He reveals the types of deference needed to stay in the system. In his private world, he conceptualizes these processes as the outcome of simply being in a ruthless industry when he talks about how he sees racism as operating within football and the structures of management:

> I think it would be naïve to say there is no racism, it would be naïve to say that bearing in mind the egotistical people that are on boards. At the moment its frightening. But Keith is doing well, Les is doing well at Bristol, they will be judged on results. Did John Barnes lose his job because of racism? No it's about results. I think it's foolish to look back and think we got the sack because we were coloured. (Shaun Watson)

Shaun's experience shows the dilemma of being in an industry where he wants to be considered as a manager without having to subscribe to any vague notions of being black, politically or culturally. Like his white manager he's content with the term 'coloured', whilst also seeing a form of white male arrogance, which he sees as a trait attached to gender rather than to their race. He also colludes with the myth that because black managers are doing well, racism, as a barrier is negated, as his first priority is to be a manager in his private world and act like a manager in his public world.

It is important to examine the origins of this belief that it is possible to achieve a position as a manager despite how racism operates inside or outside the management structure of English soccer. One of the rationales behind this self-determination can be seen in this interview with a black manager:

> I know it's difficult but I try not make the issue being black, because black people get into the ghetto and they look around and they don't see many bursting their gut to get out, you have to be different. I don't didn't want to be another person using the excuse that I am black and I can't do that. The support I would have expected from black

people wasn't there, because they are jealous. I don't think I am a sell out, but I am pro black, but I don't go and shout it from the roof top. (Steve Milk)

Steve reinforces the negative aspects of the 'white mask'; he internalizes the problem that black people use their environment as a deterrent to achieving their aspiration, that they use their blackness to as a convenient excuse. He suggests that internalizing the idea of being black leads to a lack of assertion and determination needed to escape from the ghetto. He, like the white theorists in Chapter 1, creates a pathology in the black community, which enables him to claim that to succeed you have to play down the importance of racism, but paradoxically, being black means you have to work twice as hard to succeed. Steve feels he is still able to retain his blackness by adopting a position that is silent and by having an internal sense of who he is, without shouting out that he is black:

At the end of the day people who know me, know what I am about. I am married to a white women, and my children are half caste and politically that's where I am at. They will only give you a job if we are a success, it's important for me to be successful. The likes of me have got to be successful, as at most clubs the most successful players are the black players. But if your good enough you will be employed, but we do need to be better, we have to be better, we have got to better, because if we are not better it similar to society, if we are not we will not be given a chance. (Steve Milk)

Steve, more than any of the black managers I interviewed, shows a list of contradictions that black men rarely have the luxury to discuss and reveal. Many people may jump on the political incorrectness of the narrative 'half caste', but this is a distraction from the true sentiment of his comment. Unlike John Barnes, who does not want to be judged professionally in relation to his private world, Steve's orientation to this world of management is very much linked to his external world. In his relationship with a white woman and his mixed parentage children, he no longer has any attachment to a defined notion of having to be black. The contradiction here is that he still feels an obligation to be successful, despite then going on to measure success for black people as having to be 'better' than their white male counterparts. The repetitive theme in Steve's talk is the central contradiction that black people should not make their blackness an issue, but then because of being black they have to be better, work harder, and not even consider that racism may play any part in their destiny.

Ironically, whilst I was completing this book Steve was sacked as the manager of Stockport due to poor results, and some argue he should have been sacked earlier but for the fear of the club being accused of being racist. In this assumption we can re-examine how the race game is played out in the management structure. One of the central and perennial fears of employing a black manager is that white men expose themselves to the accusation of being racist. This issue of the false accusation based on race makes it more difficult to distinguish what racism is as unconscious or conscious actions and unforeseen outcomes. There was a debate in the English game after Paul Davis at Arsenal was denied promotion to an Under-17 academy post, because he was seen as too laid back, which reflects the historical and current stereotypes that have plagued black men outside the sporting context. It is epitomized by the ongoing contradictory perception of black men as either laid back or, on the other hand, outspoken, as revealed in an article by Ian Wright in the *Daily Express* of 18 September 2003 when he says 'I knew I would not be England boss, I'm outspoken and black' and went on to comment:

> As much as you say we're progressing, we ain't progressing if you know what I mean. It as much as they want to let you progress. What I mean is that football is just like society, the Establishment let you progress as much as they want to, and no more.

Black managers consequently mirror an industry that requires them to keep their private and public worlds separate. But Ian Wright breaks this tradition, and more critically suggests the movement of black manager is outside of that manager's control. Whether they are perceived as either outspoken or laid back, it is the establishment that determines who is allowed to enter. Wright is often perceived as the Malcolm X of the soccer world. He refuses to be the 'house nigger'; he does not want to be dependent on the white man for a job in this industry, but he knows they control this environment and dictate his progression.

This view is disputed by the recent response made by Chris Kamara, now a presenter at Sky Television. Like Viv Anderson, Chris has often been reputed to defend the action of white men, to denounce racism, to advocate a level playing field. For example, in the *Sun* of 27 September 2003, p. 8:

> So when it comes to this burning issue, yes there is discrimination in football. But certainly not all of it is racial. And not to the extent some would have you believe. If you persevere and work hard, something will turn up. And it will no matter what your skin colour is.

Chris's comment again must be read as one of the many different ways in which black ex-players conceptualize racism. Here its absent, but implicit in this statement is the theme of having to work twice as hard. More dangerously, access is still based on the assumption that 'something will turn up'.

The sum effect is that Chris and other black ex-players struggle in different ways to be liberated, to be judged as individuals rather than as black men who have to fit into white men's social world. The strategies they use to operate in a world of white men, whilst maintaining their own identity, are rooted in different histories and will not always be same. The sum total of their different experiences and their different approaches to being black managers reveals an industry in which they cannot simply act in a one-dimensional way through the adoption of the 'white mask'. There is a need for a private world in which black ex-players can make sense of what is going on in their lives in the industry, where they are unable to reflect back to white men who fail to grant them the same privileges that come with being a white manager. Consequently black managers have to find a space outside the pressures to conform to white men's expectations, where they are free and able to be themselves, even if that freedom is based on a variety of identities that are not the same.

The outcome of this process of internal conversation is that black players have a range of options that are much more liberating than the constraints of the 'white mask'. Although the industries in which white men have control may not change, black men who become managers can begin to manipulate the label of being a black manager at those points of time when the two processes, being black and being a manager, constrain them. The real accomplishment for black managers is to relegate the need for the title 'black manager' and to be seen and judged simply as managers. This is not a denial of their identity as black men, but rather a position of empowerment in that they do not feel the need for a 'white mask'. They do not need a 'white mask' to assist them in the process of resolving, in their private world, that they have to be white to be accepted.

My plea on behalf of black ex-players who become managers is that their abilities and potentials as managers should not be measured by assumptions based upon their race. This represents an injustice within a system that reduces their abilities to their blackness, rather than simply considering them as individual men trying to become part of the existing management structure. Consequently any requirement to change is always perceived as the responsibility of black managers, because collectively they are the ones who are considered to be different, although these assumed differences are never named. As a result the aim of the 'white mask' should be to mirror white men's actions and expectations into the public world, to challenge their racism into achieving concrete action to change the ways they both perceive and restrict the opportunities of black men making the transition into management. Unfortunately white men are continually let off the hook in their relationships with black men who try to become managers as they simply don't see the barriers they create in this process.

–5–

'It Ain't Half White Mum':
Whiteness as a Professional Culture

In terms of institutional racism, nobody tells you they are discriminating against you, the culture of the organization makes you know where your place is. As a black person you have got to know that part of British culture means that you are trying to co-exist with a group of norms that you are grappling with. The people within that world will manipulate processes to suit themselves; they appoint people in their own image. White people are still at the top, white people still have the power. (Sir Herman Ouseley, Chair of the Commission for Racial Equality, interview, 1997)

As Ouseley reveals, it is important to look at how white men 'manipulate processes' and 'appoint people in their image' through their very ordinary acts, which give meaning to whiteness within their organizations. This is similar to the work carried out by Ware and Back (2001):

One area of research opened up by the recent focus on whiteness entails questioning ordinary people on a range of topics designed to draw out their perception of what it means to be white in different social and geographical locations. (Ware and Back, 2001: 8)

From this analysis I suggest that white men do not easily perceive or even want to consider that they are privileged in being white and that this privilege is reinforced by their gender, the powerful combination of being white and male, although to a far lesser extent women have increased their level of power in the last few years. But crucially it is white men who take for granted the power of being white and this is reflected in the institutions in which they work and live. Consequently in the structures of soccer the fight for a level playing field, for a colour-blind ethos, has not begun. The most important process is 'how does whiteness as a form of racism take place inside soccer'? More specifically how the privileges that come with being white materialize through the talk, actions and forms of consciousness of white men as the foundations on which the industry is based. It is vital to deconstruct how a colour-blind philosophy works in favour of white men who operate without being held accountable to whiteness as a political colour. Whiteness is a process by which white men cannot see the barriers facing black ex-players or how their actions contribute to institutional forms of white-ness:

> The routine normal activity of whiteness and the often camouflaged structures of priv-ileges extended to those categorised as white compared to the notion of institutional-ized racism which serves to prevent those citizens outside of the category from enjoying equal rights and opportunities in a nominally democratic society. (Ware and Back, 2001: 8)

I see the privileges of whiteness as embodied through the ways by which white men act and perform in their locations, and in their lives outside these locations, which are closely linked. This leads to a comfort zone, where conversation is not necessary, but where forms of racism and exclusion can be detected by observing white men in action with other white men and in the interface with the outsider. It is important to analyse how white personnel, through their mundane and everyday actions, develop an institutional culture that manifests the patterns of inclusion and exclusion that are faced by black and Asian men. Offside racism represents the behind-the-closed-door acts that cannot be flagged up, because white men cannot see either racism in the system or the role they play in the structures in perpetuating forms of inequality. This is a form of racism by which white men refute any direct responsibility for the moral panic surrounding institutional racism, which limits the possibility of changing the outcomes of their actions in the structures of football.

White Male Denial through Talk

> Howard suffered from a black man's attitude towards the white man. See, everybody thinks whites have got a problem with blacks. In reality blacks have got a problem with whites. Howard unfortunately was the only black man, nobody got on with him, and he thought he was the only one to get it. I am not prejudiced, but if a coloured moved in next door I'd move out like most white people would. If my daughter came home with a nigger I'd go mad. (Tommy Smith, quoted in Hill, 1989: 89).

Tommy Smith asserts the idea that Howard Gayle, as a black man, is unable to assimilate into his environment, which he has, as a white player, constructed as his comfort zone, where he reveals a vulnerability by his need to hold on to his superi-ority. He sees the pathology and the need for change as the black player's responsi-bility as his resistance to a black man to living next door, or polluting his race by going out with his daughter, brings Tommy's social world into the context of the culture of playing. It is an ideology formed around the belief that black men may threaten his professional and institutional world, and may disrupt the traditions on which his life has been based. Racism, in this situation, represents the failure to change and the fear of the arrival of black players who may alter this privilege that he has taken for granted. This theme of white men maintaining their privileges by depicting black men as problematic is revealed in this account from a white manager:

> They have been brainwashed. Maybe they were innocently being exploited for racist purposes. The second generation were hell-bent on stirring up the whole unsavoury atmosphere again. I saw it as reverse racism, the minority came into the game, brash and swaggering and full of arrogance, like the world owed them a living, simply because they were born black. (Atkinson 1998: 167)

Atkinson (1998) reveals a contradictory position as a white man, who, on the one hand has worked, managed and co-existed alongside black players, yet, when they challenge his reality, he's disorientated. He articulates an unconscious arrogance that establishes his power over black players by suggesting they should not question his status and the institutions in which he works. Here racism moves to an emotional form when white men are threatened; it becomes fragile and confused, and ultimately defensive. This is demonstrated through his assumption that black men should not act above their station, as Atkinson (1998) depoliticizes the power of black players who have no rights in his world as a white man, at the moment when he can no longer control them. The implications for Atkinson (1998) are that the links between individual and institutional forms of racism are disguised by his failure to see that his beliefs about black players lead to forms of discrimination in the structures where he operates. More crucially, Atkinson (1998) expresses an assumed consensus amongst white men that resonates outside society – despite his reference to them being 'lazy niggers' in 2004 – that they cannot be racist if they have worked with and employed black people, based upon the historical notion, that 'some of his best friends are black'. It is a powerful and rational form of whiteness because it does not consider the power dynamics when black people in general and black players inside sport question their marginalized position. To open up these forms of denial and look at how racism is an ordinary, everyday means of deflecting attention away from white men, it is important to recognize that white men are not aware of these moments when they unconsciously reveal this confusion, that they can both tolerate difference and feel threaten by it, preferring to chose their 'own':

> If I am recruiting somebody I would look at the standards. I would not look at the colour. If I was a manager and I needed an assistant, it may be, well, it would not be a black person I would choose, because most of my contacts in the game or the people I know aren't black. But it wouldn't be because they are black. It would be who I know and what standard they are at. (Tom Franklin)

The problem of white men not seeing how their beliefs have consequences for institutions is illustrated during this interview with a director of coaching for a famous west London team. His explanation of how his working-class background would lead him to select a white, working-class man, reveals a lack of awareness of unconsciously choosing to employ someone who resembles his own background. The assumption that this is not a process of racism needs to be questioned, because irrespective of his intent, the outcome is that it is his favouritism for his 'own' that alienates and discriminates against a category of people, based on race, who are not privileged to benefit from being part of his social world.

When I asked a white, south London coach, now a prominent member of the national England team's coaching staff, about his identity as a white man, he responded:

> No, I don't think of myself as a white coach, I don't think I need to do that. I have read articles about black coaches, who feel they need to call themselves black coaches, maybe that's something about black culture, and not selling out in being seen as white. (Frank Jones)

Frank talked openly about his teaching background in a multiracial school and acknowledged the fact that if he had not been white, he would have found it even more difficult to rise to his present position in a mercenary profession like football. Through this comment we can begin to see the privilege of not having to identify the codes that makes his power transparent, whilst black players are seen to form their identity in relation to the power he renders invisible, simply being a white man. The need for change is continually rooted in the direction of black players in different areas of the industry from their point of arrival into the game:

> I think that young black players entering the game needed to have convinced people in the game that they were white men with black skins. They would have to adjust to the whole culture of the game from dressing room banter, through to the way they dressed, the way they acted. I think with young Afro-Caribbean players coming in and in their own way and rather confronting white traditions, they changed them and introduced some of their own background and culture, which leads to a change in a particular club if not the game. (Frank Jones)

The dressing room is an important reference point for whiteness forming through the processes of dress, social activities, and more specifically the power of humour to which black players had to accommodate. Black players thus very subtly reach a new point of inverting some of the traditions that have been taken for granted by white players. In this case whiteness is reframed by black players, but without any powerful costs in challenging the customs that underwrite the power of white men. The dressing room is a site where processes of inclusion are enacted by white men who are never held accountable for the pressures they place on black men to conform. Consequently white men unconsciously do not realize that white identity is formed in these relationships, which are continually reflected in a culture to which black players have to adjust.

Whiteness, as a form, is further influenced by class, as illustrated in this next comment by a white manager at his exclusive Surrey tennis club:

> You look at this tennis club that we are in today, there's not a coloured person in sight, so there is a part of society where they don't mix in well, or they are not a part of. They will do things with a bit of flair, possibly a white person wouldn't do, and that's a generalization, but I think their natural instinct is to have a go at something. I think they are prepared to chance their arm at something, you know they will try something that's not always safety first. (Andrew Smooth)

Andrew's comment presents caricatures of black players as different, unpredictable and unable to assimilate. This view is similar to the theories discussed in Chapter 1, in that black players lack intelligence and are impulsive and unplanned. His conceptualization is kept private by the location, excused by the getting out phrase 'generalization' in a place when there are no black people around to challenge his views. Whiteness is formed in these unpressurized moments. The location is vital: it is a similar to other closed spaces in society in which Andrew assumes that whiteness just happens. It is an unspoken norm.

Embodied and Unconscious Forms of Racism in White Men

Processes of spoken, white male denial manifest themselves in a variety of different ways in comparison to the embodied forms of whiteness that can be seen in the ways that white men perform in their structures. In this first case I focus on the Football Association, the governing body for the game in England, which is responsible for promoting and developing football and is accountable to the Football Association Council. The Football Association, as an establishment, has developed its structure over a 100-year period, where all ninety-two of its committee members are white, with only one woman. The committee structure therefore embodies a form of whiteness that leads to the inclusion solely of white people, in both its committee and occupational structures.

I interviewed one social actor, the ex-technical director of the coaching department, to see him at work in his location and to reveal whiteness as a form that changes in contradictory ways. I sat in the waiting room at Lancaster Gate, the then offices of the Football Association, with a black female colleague, and we were invited to start the interview. From the stark expression of this white man it was clear that he had not realized that we were black. He was neatly dressed in a dark blue suit, appearing perturbed and uneasy as he tried to be polite whilst responding nervously to my questions about his route into his position in the Football Association. His embarrassed laughter, the lack of eye contact and the way he continually banged his pen against the desk indicated to me that his world has been disrupted by the entry of two unknown, black people, with whom he was not familiar with.

He talked coyly about his time at Loughborough University, his two children, and the impressive changes he had made in the Football Association structure. His attempts to be charming and to gain creditability in the audience of two black people, by accounts of his friendships with other black people in the profession, reflected one moment of whiteness as cautious, when its comfort zone is disorientated. His conclusion that black people needed to change before his organization could begin to accommodate them reinforces the theme of white men as reluctant to adjust to differences because of the challenge and possible changes to both their heritage and cultural world. A contradiction is revealed, in that it is possible to perform a belief in equality, which is then undermined by the suggestion that black men are not equal to the task of working within his setting.

This contradiction between performances of equality and white men's actual beliefs was further demonstrated when I returned to the Football Association with two new white personnel. One of these white men was a leading figure from the Regional Sports Council and the other was the liaison officer for the Sports Council in relation to the Football Association. The tone and atmosphere of this meeting was completely different, the warmth was now converted to a hostility and disrespect towards me. The meeting revealed how whiteness and masculinity can change its form in the presence of one black man who has no power, and in the absence of a black women, enabling white men to act without the pressures of gender influences. These dynamics presented themselves in the following ways. I was placed in between these two white men, on a lower chair. The technical director had brought his secretary to take notes. He looked directly into the eyes of the two white men and in a harsh tone, made explicit his personal and organizational views on racism in the Football Association:

> You know there are no problems with racism in this organization; we have many women working here. If black people are not making the break through, then they need to look at themselves. There are too many people around trying to make a career out of making trouble. I got here through sheer hard work and endeavour; I didn't come from a privilege family setting. (Terry Williams, Technical Director of the Football Association)

The force of this declaration had not been possible in the previous meeting when he had been confronted with two black people in the absence of these white men. This comment demonstrates that Terry does not have to think about whether or not he is being disrespectful. He is now back in a comfort zone as he tries to safeguard his position, controlling his environment, his routines and his ways of being in his organization by deflecting racism as being 'out there'. More specifically in the lives of the white men around him at this moment he can now depict the problem of racism as based upon black men's paranoia. His reaction is thus a defence to a real fear that he is being attacked, but he is now able to be openly rude in the presence of two white men whom he knows will not challenge him or tell other people about his conduct. The outcome of this collusion is that he can condemn a black man whom he perceives as challenging his goodwill by questioning his commitment to tackle racism on his terms. He knows instinctively that the other white men will collude with his actions through their silence, thus demonstrating their implicit loyalty and keeping this act private and undisclosed. These acts of collusion operate unconsciously amongst these white men, sanctioned by past relationships in buildings occupied by white men in similar suits, very similar to what happens in other organizational cultures in British society. Despite white men's different personalities, they fail to see, or take the risk of flagging up, these moments of race collaboration, revealed here by the failure of one of the white men present to name and confront the manner in which this white man abused this power at the time it took place, casually remarking, 'he's always like that'.

The failure to look at whiteness as a performance that can be offensive means that the actions of the white actors become acceptable inside the structures of football, as part of the professional norm of whiteness.

In the next example, embodied acts of racism could be seen in a more contradictory way. I was invited back to the London Football Association to see the performances of a new technical director. Instead of going with a black woman I was accompanied by a white male. We went to discuss a proposal to increase the participation of black players in management. The meeting had the potential to explore – through my role as secretary of the Martin Shaw King Trust and my role as a researcher – how racism operates dependent on the context and the personnel.

We arrived together. I was dressed formally, all in black, attempting to blend, to be accredited into whiteness by my suit and tie and smart black shoes. My colleague, on the other hand, turned up in jeans and a short jacket. We were greeted by a white receptionist, who welcomed me using my surname, and my colleague using his title and status – doctor. This was the first example of a different approach taken toward us as black and white men, despite how we dressed – a deference was automatically given to being white. We were then taken up to the second floor and directed into the office of the new technical director, who was formally dressed in a suit and tie. For two hours he lectured us, directing most of his eye contact towards my white friend, relegating my presence to that of a spectator. This was the second example of deference towards being white, although viewing it as such could be translated as another form of black paranoia. We were told stories about Andy Cole, as the technical director mimicked how Cole would 'kiss his teeth' in his response to white coaches. He controlled the interview by the pitch of his voice, closed responses to open questions and delaying tactics, saying he would get back to us about the FA's response to equality standards in their organization.

The interview revealed another contradiction in the performances of white men – the luxury of being verbally committed to supporting the development of black players, whilst simultaneously demonstrating racist charicatures and behaving in a demeaning way towards a black researcher. It's important to recognize that these acts are not static. They can change from moment to moment, depending upon the different types of actors who are present.

These complexities can be further exposed by considering the arrival of the new chief executive to the Football Association, whom I was fortunate to meet in the presence of a black male colleague and an Asian male representative from the communication department of the Football Association. Although white men in this kind of situation may appear outnumbered, they still hold the power. It is their home and their structures that are being criticized. What was contradictory in this third example was the different approaches being taken by this white man in a senior position in this organization:

> You must remember the Football Association has not been very good in communicating what it does. Most people still think its about giving fines out and taking peoples money way. One thing we have not been very good at is trying to bring new faces in, not just black faces but young people and women. There are some committees who start the meeting by reading out who has died from the last meeting. I know there is a major problem with our council and our county structure and we may have to short-circuit them to get more black faces. (Chief Executive FA, interview, 2002)

Here we see and hear the changing face and voices of whiteness, moving from a close and suspicious position, to one that is openly critical and challenging, without naming the actors involved in the exclusion of black people in the Football Association structure. Although in the presence of these black men the dynamics change, what emerges is a Labour-type spin, a twenty-first century liberalism, which may seem more progressive than the approach of his previous colleague, but was without any commitment to change the structure, only to short-circuit it, to make it easier for black people to get in. The danger is that race is put into the widening category of other equity issues, like age and gender, thus diluting the singular and individual problems that black people experience. The specifics of the problems that confront black men in the transition in the administrative structures of English soccer become more disguised during these moments when white men are not given time to prepare and plan their responses.

The issue of the impulsive nature of whiteness was tested at a public, open level when I attended the launch of the South London Initiative, a joint Partnership between the south London football clubs to tackle racism in football in 1997. The launch was held at Football, Football in Piccadilly and several weeks previously I had spoken to the Sports Minister, Tony Banks, for several minutes at a European conference against racism at Manchester United Football Club. We met again at this launch at Football, Football, and I asked if he remembered me. He responded: 'Of course I know who you are, did you think I thought you were Ruud Gullit?'

He then pulled my locks very hard, smiled and walked over to join the chairman of the Commission for Racial Equality. The place was very crowded and extremely noisy, but a black male and black female colleague had witnessed this event in total shock and disbelief as a clear form of onside racist abuse. We looked at each other in total bewilderment. Our anger was so acute and disorientating that we did not know whether to risk disclosing this act. To make it public as the first step, to use this white man as an example of white male racism, would damage any future work in this area. I stood in my blue suit and tie, sweating, unable to move, whilst this person casually walked off, totally oblivious of his action.

I decided instead to write to this political figure to explore on a one-to-one level how he understood his actions and was invited to a meeting at the House of Commons. I went with my supervisor, who is white and male and was involved in conducting similar researches into processes of racism in football, again to compare our experiences of how racism operates in this setting. We were met by the Sports Minister's secretary and were taken to the garden outside to wait for the Minister. The Minister arrived 10 minutes later, dressed in a smart Next suit. He sat opposite me, smiled, and offered me a drink. My supervisor sat opposite the Minister's secretary, who is also white. I realized I was not only outnumbered, but again inside a different zone of whiteness. The minister then apologized for his behaviour, with a false grin, but he had failed to realize how he had offended me by amusingly implying that all black people looked the same or, more unconsciously, the disrespect he had shown for the heritage of Rastafarian traditions by pulling my locks. But he then discredited the apology by suggesting that I misunderstood this gesture, thus producing another example of a deflection of racism that again views the problem as one of paranoia and of black people being oversensitive. His actions and comment had shown me the types of abuse and stereotyping a black outsider may have to endure in order to gain inside access to white men's unconscious racism in their professional context. As I walked out of the House of Commons I realized that, to open up these processes, I had to perform in similar ways to the black players and black manager in relation to this white man's standards. I had to show I was not a threat, to make him feel comfortable, to be himself inside his space, to make sense of whiteness as an embodied process.

Race Cognizance and White Male Guilt

It is important to look at how white men in football reveal a form of whiteness through guilt, which is so debilitating as an emotion that they are unable to implicate themselves in the process of racism. This is a form of race cognizance in which feeling guilty about being white and what it represents in terms of discrimination does not mean that white men understand how their actions contribute towards patterns of exclusion. During an interview with a football chairman I was interested in how this white man understood the privilege of his whiteness and how he saw himself as the victim of racism which meant he could not be a perpetrator. We met in his office just before a big promotion match. He looked anxious and was distracted by a number of telephone calls during the interview, as he responded to my question about why he, as a white man, had been able to become a chairman of a football club:

> Without any culture or race, the outsider has to work harder. I was born in China and was the only white man I had to work harder, and blacks have been here for fifty years and coming into the next century I would love to see better race relations and black people don't have to become white to be accepted. I mainly got into my position because of money and working hard to get this club off the ground. (Mark Brent)

Mark's conception of himself as white whilst in the minority, suggests this difference motivated him to succeed. When in the majority position as a white man within the context of the football club, he suggests black people do not have to be motivated by being different to be accepted into the structures of football. The problem is that white men can succeed based on one moment of thinking about their whiteness whilst black people have to constantly think about what it is to be black over this 50-year period. This is because this white man underestimates the privileges he has as a white man in controlling the pace in which race equality takes place, whereever he is. Unfortunately Mark's perception of himself as a white 'victim' does not lead to a cognizance of the specifically different problems and conditions facing black people seeking representation in his structures inside his country. He can feel guilty about the moral effects of racism, as something that is bad, without having to see that his own whiteness is the product of how he lives his life in his organization and his social world despite his avowed approach to anti-racism. Consequently his guilt can operate without resulting in any change in his internal reckoning and without recognition of the power he has as a white man. He can continue to exist in an industry and a political world where there are race barriers and race exclusion, without having to think about the need to change his life to accommodate the problems black people may experience in finding a place in his organization:

> I am not actively saying come on board we need a black person, I think it will emerge. I tell you the route it might come from, through the supporters club. I personally don't know any black guy with £700,000 quid in the business going spare. I don't know any black guys, but having said that, there is a BMW dealer, but he is a bloody rugby fan.

It's a black family and half of them are from Gloucester, it's strange seeing a black guy with a Gloucester accent. I don't think the majority of Chairmen are racist; it's an issue of time rather than race. I always consider the Northern clubs to be the most fascist. (Mark Brent, Chairman of Charlton Football Club)

The comment highlights how this white man can exempt himself from addressing the more complex task of assessing to what extent the lack of black representation in his boardroom may be rooted within exclusive racist processes in his private and public life. So he does not have to campaign publically for black people's entry – he can suggest they have a role but outside the legitimate route, through the supporters section, which has very little political power in his organization. Consequently his aversion to seeing the specific historical problems of black people limits him from seeing that the black BMW owner has been alienated from the tradition of whiteness despite the fact he has the money and has a 'Gloucester accent'. Money is not the issue; this is a person he does not know who does not fit in his perceptions of the personal qualities to operate within his boardroom. More critically, by establishing that northern clubs operate more overt onside forms of fascism than the racism taking place within his own sphere, he tries to exonerate himself from being implicated in any real practices of exclusion. The impact is that he displaces racism, which leads to a distraction over how he is actually responsible for the barriers that prevent black people entering into the structures of football. This fatalism leads to a feeling that 'nothing can be done', 'change is impossible' because racism is difficult to relate to as a real act. Consequently racism cannot be identified or eliminated because of the way it is positioned as an invisible part of 'the things we are', so disguising the more complex processes by which white men enter the structures of sport and colonize them.

White guilt, as a form of denial of racism, can also lead to a position where white men overidentify with the victims of exclusion, black players, by assuming that they can have some form of 'racialized empathy'. I am using 'racialized empathy' to describe the ways in which white men, because of their guilt, feel that they understand and have had similar experiences of exclusion to black players in the system. This notion of 'racialized empathy' can be seen to be operating in this comment by a white Scottish man, a leading figure from the Scottish Professional Football Association. He was responding to my question about institutionalized racism in the organization of soccer and the inevitable dominance of white men in these structures:

The mentality of white people in institutional settings is very white, very rarely do they mix or understand people who are not white and British. I am sure if I was a black person I would not have got into the position I am in today. That's because of the mentality of the people who run the game, it's a security thing and they go for people who are like us, they tend to think that white people understand the British mentality better than black people. (Terry Hill)

This text seems insightful of the black experience of discrimination and is also an apology for a historical tradition where this white man sees his faults are entrenched in the way white men in the past have not wanted to be around people who are not white or British. He captures the problem of the failure of white men to connect with black people in the social world, which is mirrored in the context of sport. Whiteness, from this perspective, is not taking the risk of letting outsiders in who might expose the foundation on which their closeted racism is built. This is a form of insecurity by which white men can feel vulnerable and threatened by the possibility of being around black men who see and experience the culture of their sport as unwelcoming. Whiteness is objectified as British, so excusing this Scottish man who now has a shared enemy, he is no longer white at this moment, as British white racism is a completely different phenomena. He thus becomes the 'honorary black man'. Terry can render his power as a white man in an abstract way without having to name the specific role he takes in perpetuating the patterns of discomfort that exclude black men. He can attempt to redress the privilege of being white in a broad way by trying to be anti-racist and can then exempt himself from addressing how forms of race inequality are created through his own actions. Terry can still sympathize with the black player's plight without having to change personally.

It is important, in this next example from the chief executive of the League Managers Association, to examine more directly how white men assume the issues and problems of getting black players to come into their whiteness:

We want more coloured people coaching for obvious reasons; the relationship between coloured people and coloured coaches is one reason. Perhaps coloured lads think they would not be able to control these fellows. Any coloured lad in the game should be saying I want to coach with him, my recommendation to any coloured lad coming into the game is that they should set their stall out to network. (Barry West)

Barry reveals a form of whiteness that unconsciously implies that black players are less able, despite his intention to tackle racism in his institution and explore the possibility of their involvement. This potential involvement reduces the role of black players in the white structures of soccer to offering empathy for other black players; it simply assumes that black people automatically understand other black people, that they are a homogenous and unified group without distinction. Implicit in this statement is a system that emerges unconsciously by which white men assume that black men lack the competence to manage other white men. They are safe and more assertive in command of their own. Whilst this white man sees the need for black representation at a very low level, he can also prevail inside these structures of football, as sites of white, male culture, which escape scrutiny as processes of racialized exclusion. White men can patronize black players, suggesting that they are wanted, as long as they do not effect radical changes in the structures or take their jobs. The word 'coloured' dates the mentality of the comment to a colonial age. It depoliticizes the issue from one of representation to one of integration, more specifically the assimilation of the outsider into a world where they might not be able to cope with.

This form of whiteness operates on a different level in the context of the union structure for the players, through the Professional Footballers Association (PFA). This organization is formed around ex-players representing players, based upon a structure of a chief executive, deputy chief executive and a committee structure. Its purpose is to represent the needs of all its players irrespective of race and culture. The following quotation is from an interview with the chief executive of the PFA:

> We are much more comfortable when we've got a fair percentage of black players. They have been quite insular, not to say arrogant and aloof, who say we should be stronger. For the Football Association, you would struggle to see a black face, particularly in council, in administration and in coaching. It is hard enough when you're black, but the likes of Viv Anderson have become coaches/managers, but you can count them on one hand. It is a situation we are duty bound to change. (Sam King)

When asked about the role and positioning of black players Sam acknowledged the importance of their inclusion into his structure but in two conflicting ways. Firstly, he almost demonized them as difficult, regarding their delay as being due to self-exclusion. Secondly, we see again the classical method of displacement. By being critical of exclusions in other structures in football, the PFA is an innocent bystander, an ally of the black cause because of the brotherhood of players from different races playing alongside each other. This brotherhood breaks down on the issue of competition for jobs, where his support for black players is based upon the notion that they have special needs and not that they are victims of institutionally racist processes. Consequently, black players in the industry are perceived as needing help, rather than there being a need to address problems they experience in the system. This means that the PFA can celebrate its achievement in attempting to involve more black faces, whilst the conditions under which they come into soccer do not change. The impact of this type of white guilt is that, yet again, it removes the need for self-analysis about how individual and institutional forms of whiteness are connected. This organizational position contains a missionary theme which black players are rescued, assisted and in need of preparation to assimilate, whilst other forms of racism, through the superiority of white men, stand apart from the process of assimilation.

What becomes apparent in these emerging forms of denial through 'guilt' is that white individuals do not concretely link their actions to the forming of an institutional culture.

Fatalism, Whiteness and Institutional Displacement

> This is a major problem that has faced English soccer as a whole; we have the tradition of the country that introduced the sport to the world. We were the first people to have the rules of the game, the first one to have a management system to control how the game is run. We have gone through a traditional English way of setting up committees and setting up councils, which is a very much an English, middle class way of doing things. It is part of the culture of middle class English men to be involved in that kind of administration, the committee method. (Frank Jones)

This comment suggests that whiteness, both historically and in the context of sport, just happens to lie outside very mundane and ordinary social relationships; it has an entrenched civilized ethic, where white people are the only ones with the intellect and capability to run the game. This assumption is the foundation upon which white men perpetuate themselves in the structures of football. It has strong political associations with the colonial racism described in Chapter 1, where whiteness is symbolic of superiority, rationality and the ability to organize. It is this uncontested form of Englishness that underpins a regime built upon the arrogance of a committee structure in which mutual forms of recognition legitimize the idea that only white men are best able to run the organization. The connections between class, race and gender are important because of the status ascribed to the white middle-class men who are trusted to administer organizations and to develop the structures in which their heritage is invested.

In this interview with Kate Hoey, then Member of Parliament for Vauxhall, it is possible to illustrate how forms of whiteness, masculinity and class operate as the focal points of inclusion:

> The problems with politics and, to a greater extent sport is that they are filled with white men, who have come out of university, or football clubs and go straight into organization without any life experiences of the difficulties of other groups. They talk as if they got there on their own merit and don't seem to realize how much easier it is for them compared to other groups. (Kate Hoey, Member of Parliament for Vauxhall in 1998, now the Sports Minister)

Kate's comment illustrates how white men fit into institutions without having to be aware of the connections between their masculinity and their whiteness, because the processes regarding their entry are never questioned. Kate, as a white woman, is able to locate and see white men acting out a form of whiteness because she has had to break down, and into, these 'comfort zones' in which whiteness is institutionalized amongst men. To connect forms of whiteness to comfort zones that lead to the privileges through the ways that white men are able to reinforce their lives into the institutions of sport I examined Sports England.

Sports England is responsible for ensuring that all sport in England operates around a set of principles concerning elitism, participation and, recently, anti-discriminatory practices (see the Sporting Equals Race Equality Charter). Sports England is headed by the Minister for Sport, appointed by Tony Blair, the Prime Minister, and, according to my interview with Phil Lee, of the South-east Region Sports Council, it is an organization made up of mainly white men between the ages of 30 and 65 years. To demystify whiteness, to make it visible through analysing the lives of the personnel in their structures, I talked to a leading figure at Sports England about his move into the arena of sports administration and the power he had, as a white man, in this structure. He also talked about the recruitment processes within his organization:

> There are still organizations in sport that don't like being challenged; it is like a relationship or a marriage. It comes down to what people look like, behave like, that influences the decision. When you get into management structures of sport and coaching structures of sport its about the existing structures selecting an individual who does not look like them and the person who does not look like them making a decision whether they want to be involved. The more you challenge the individual the more they retreat into their standard values and seeing themselves and the interaction with others so you never get through the person's barriers. And if you challenge their perceptions of themselves you challenge their consciousness, it's destabilizing and can be extremely disturbing. (Phil Lee)

The metaphor of a marriage reveals how individuals choose their partners on the basis of a resemblance to each other's histories and personalities, to the point where they end up looking like each other. Phil opens up the privileges of being white as a heritage handed down, based upon strong historical roots, in which whiteness is invisible, because of the legacy of silence in which it forms it status. This is an arranged 'marriage' that is based upon a culture that appeals to a shared unconscious process of being white and male, made diverse by the different contexts and locations in which these relationships of power are negotiated. To challenge these power formations, is to challenge the institution that has been colonized by white men by closing its door to anybody who may disturb the patterns according to which they live their lives. This pattern of white men working within comfort zones with other white men is at the very core of the behaviours of institutional marriages, where white men develop ways of eating, meeting and conversing together that are never stated openly.

It is clear from this perspective that the institution is no where near ready for a mixed-race marriage, with a new generation of children who may dismantle the basis on which whiteness is formed. The metaphor of the marriage as the foundation of institutional whiteness is crucial for a society where a mixed-race relationship may be taking place, but they are not mirrored inside the institutions of football. This is the crucial challenge of the ability and the altruism of white men to develop new relationships outside of their cultural, social and racial world to the extent of sharing access to their power base.

These relationships established by white men are intrinsically linked into football structures through networks that facilitate the development of forms of racism featured by white men continually reaffirming their places in football, and into which they fail to admit outsiders. Entry into these structural relationships is determined by being a white man or being around white men and adopting the range of different behaviours and values that are attached to whiteness including denial, guilt and the embodied preconscious forms of acting white.

This comment from Phil Lee begins to show one particular way in which a form of white masculine behaviour takes place when getting a position in sports administration, weeding out individuals who have not been through a similar process:

> Well my background was in water sports. I went into racing in a big way. I took part in the world and Olympic championships, did a PE course on retirement, then a sports development course, and then went to the sports council. But you do tend to find that most people at the Sports Council are qualified people from white middle class backgrounds, against those people who have the hands on experience. They are usually all over fifty, it's not just a change in their attitudes it's a change in their working methods. (Phil Lee)

What emerges in this comment is that some of these features of white middleclass identities are invested in systems that become rigid and cannot be penetrated. They are made functional by an assumed competence in which only those people who devise the systems can run them. These processes of doing the sport, getting qualified and having experiences unrelated to the real world of sport are the products of white male networks, where the privilege of acting on the white men's terms governs access, and reinforces the stereotype that mainly white men have the right kind of social breeding and intelligence. The idea that white men, in the organizational settings of soccer, have a shared history allows them to co-exist as long as they do not disrupt the agreed way of working upon which the organizations are founded.

Sports England then differs in terms of forms of whiteness, from other organizational cultures in the structures of football. What is consistent is a shared form of whiteness in which white men operate in structures without having to acknowledge that they are white or older, English, middle-class men. A culture of whiteness develops structurally through the status attached to being white and being male and is perpetuated through these ongoing working relationships. For white men, to challenge whiteness would mean questioning their realties and running the risk of losing these privileges. It would mean disrupting a way of working and living, which may be far too damaging, both politically and economically.

The central question, which is never asked, of whether whiteness is a psychotic state that has no insight into the reality of being white, is crucial because it takes the pathology away from those who cannot integrate because they are seen as too different. The psychosis emerges and can be assessed when white men's performances and languages are made visible and the outcomes of their actions are revealed, especially the heath-and-safety implications for men who are not white: the psychological problems the outsiders face in being rejected, and the general cultural problems or being written off as a race of people. White men who escape this type of examination can then colonize the structures of sport by not having to think about the powers of simply being male and white and being able to recite anti-racist sentiments whilst expressing racist views when their position is threatened.

They can feel guilty for how black people are affected by forces of racism outside society, through the well-worn cliché 'football mirrors society' without having to implicate themselves as part of the process throughout the different spheres of football. So, ironically, racism can exist in sport, but the mirror it reflects from outside society cannot be seen, it lives in a void because nobody wants to call it, and say clearly that the way white men act is the way they have been encouraged to act and allowed to get away with both in and outside the sporting context.

It is vitally important that to understand whiteness in the context of sport is the first step towards relinquishing its power. If we continue to see football as a self-contained, disconnected industry we do a grave injustice to the mammoth task facing black people in and outside of the game, who need to see that their pathologies are not the central intricate rationale for their exclusion. They must understand that whiteness is a phenomena that has an historical base and travels in disguise in the many worlds outside of football. They have to travel in and through these worlds without knowing the power of its presence. The denial of entry to people who cannot share or take advantage of what it is to be white is a social injustice and a political democratic issue, and not simply about role models or evolution, or the system's need for the right type of black person.

–6–

'Anti-racism can Seriously Damage Your Health': Asians as the New White Man in the League Table of Race Relations inside Football

> THE PROBLEM OF THE TWENTIETH CENTURY is the problem of the colour-line, the relation of the darker to the lighter races of men in Asia and Africa, in America and the islands of the sea. It was a phrase of this problem that caused the Civil War.
>
> Du Bois, *Souls of a Black Folk.*

I am concerned that the new wave of anti-racism inside football is not really addressing the central issues that confront black players trying to make the transition into coaching and management. We are now entering into a twenty-first century sports climate overwhelmed since the mid 1990s by an agenda to categorize individuals in terms of race, culture and nationality. Du Bois' (1903) comments allude to this danger – more specifically the problem of colour, how the shade of one's skin has important implications for one's prospects and positioning in the international world. Large numbers of people from both Asia and especially Africa are located in the English game in a complex emergence of a league table of race relations. This league table finds its rationale in the murder of Steven Lawrence by four white men in 1993, leading to an institutional obsession, almost compulsion, to implement anti-racism and social inclusion. This obsession has led to rigorous attempts to reflect a multicultural ethos, thus exempting organizations from the accusation of being seen as 'institutionally racist' without addressing the real barriers that black players face in getting jobs as managers and coaches. The implication is that race has now become an eligibility criteria in terms of one's ability to move up and down various organizations. It often determines your place in the institutions, both inside and outside football. This is particularly true of the exclusionary processes that take place inside coaching and management. It has confused the boundaries between people's racial identity, both politically and culturally. Organizations perceive individuals in particular ways once they have declared their race within a tick box monitoring system where race becomes an administrative process. Gilroy explains this perennial problem of racial classification in this comment below:

> The political language of identity levels out distinctions between chosen connections and given particularities: between the people you choose to be and the things that

determine our individuality by being thrust upon you. It is particularly important for the argument that follows that the term 'identity' has become a significant element in contemporary conflicts over cultural, ethnic, religious, 'racial' and national differences. (Gilroy 2000: 106)

Using Gilroy's (2000) comment we can see how race monitoring has created a paradoxical situation where it is now more important for excluded groups to be colour-specific, to name themselves in terms of race and national categories, but to be colour-blind to become head of the football family that makes whiteness vague as a form of power.

The earlier chapters in this book demonstrated that because of white men's failure to disclose their identity and their privileges as white men, to make whiteness transparent, they remain top of the exclusive league table of race, in terms of positions of coaches, managers and administrators. Below this premier league there is a struggle amongst a number of emerging racial and national groups to be promoted into that club. To win a point in relation to being promoted into this division depends on a variety of internal and external factors in the world of soccer and the different ways the game of race is played. These racial and cultural struggles can be compared to Roediger's (1991) work on the similar contests that took place after slavery for racial groups to obtain the privileges that went with being white. Roediger (1991) described the pressure for new racial groups after the abolition of the slave period to battle for social justice and civil rights right up to the 1960s within the promotion of the America dream.

In the context of English soccer, the murder of Steven Lawrence symbolically has created a similar atmosphere of anti-racism as the new metaphor for civil rights in the context of English society and English soccer. It has created a culture in which the language and sentiments of anti-racism have made it ever more impossible to detect the forms of racism that took place behind the closed doors of English soccer. A range of measures from the Macpherson Report (1999), Kick it Out 1993, Eliminating Racism in Football Task Report, The Football Association Equity Plan and Sporting Equals Race Equality Charter have enabled organizations to embrace the language of anti-racism. Ironically, whilst in the world outside sport, anti-racism and equity became obsolete in organizations like social services, mental health and the public care arena, 20 years on the same ineffective policies and procedures have now entered into the world of sport. This has lead to moral declarations to challenge racism and an attempt to promote and integrate new, previously absent groups that may threaten the privilege white men hold in the high positions in the sport:

If you look at the whole anti-racist experience, take it out of the context of football and look at politics, the experiences may be the same, the outcomes may be the same. In many ways the Asians don't have a figure in the game, they don't have some one to articulate their issues. There are black players, black people in the media, Garth Crooks was in the PFA, but these are processes of disenfranchisement and it relies on part-time ambassadors, but I don't have the power, I am not even part of the organization to do that. (Fred Needle)

Fred very poignantly links the world of politics and exclusion to the context of sport and soccer, and connects these origins to correct the lack of representation or to change the culture of the soccer, but also to elevate the Asian presence, to make an absent group visible, as a marker of football's attempt to genetically engineer a new multicultural perspective. The latent implication of this action has been to perceive Asians and black British-born players as two distinct groups, one group inside with power and apparently represented, the Asian group outside the whole new league table of race inside soccer. This means there is no pressure to redress the barriers facing black men. They are inside and doing OK, although in the outside world to sport they face different process or discrimination and exclusion. The ideology behind these different experiences in relation to soccer can be articulated through the film *Bend it like Beckham* (2001), which exposed a sport colluding with and reinforcing a whole set of historical and cultural stereotypes that ensured that Asians would have to be sponsored through completely different cultural league tables.

As Bains and Sanjiev (1998) reveal, the physical, religious and educational images of Asian footballers had placed them in mysteriously different processes of assimilation to other racial groups, particularly the black British with whom they are often contrasted:

> The difference between black and Asians: everything would point to a connection broadly in terms of exclusion and discrimination. I am very careful to draw a line down the middle because they are different experiences, one community are seen as shop owners and shop traders. PE teachers show more of an indifference to an Asian player than they would to a white or black player. You don't see comparable role models in the Asian community, you start to build some images in your mind and I think the negative stereotypes lead to the exclusion of Asians from the game. (Bains and Sanjiev 1998)

Bains demonstrates further this inherent problem of race as an artificial comparison and the corresponding danger of a league table of the outside groups struggling for a place, having to change their images, more specifically the perennial construction of the Asian shopkeeper. The devastating truth is that the forces of racism that divide these communities are disguised, as they search and aspire to be closer to the privileges that go with being white inside and outside British sport. Consequently the joke that Asians were not allowed into the world cup, because each time they got a corner, they opened a shop, is important to the way in which the institutions of soccer accommodate race characteristics as particular to where individuals can move into and how they can move through the football industry and the types of cultural and political sacrifices they have to make. In terms of a football pitch as the metaphor for how institutions operate around notions of social inclusion based on race, black players appear located up front, visible on the playing field, where it is assumed their physical presence means they are naturally placed, but also in terms of their intellectual ability. Asians are still at the back, gradually allowed to play out from this position, where they have the economic capability but their distinctly different culture is a point of fascination and also a threat to the notion of whiteness. The only people allowed to move up down the field or the institutions without reference to their racial attributes are white men, who can go where they like without the hindrance of race classification. They set up and have contributed towards this dangerous polarization of black and Asian people by a propensity to compare their experiences without recognizing that they may need to be discussed and analysed as different phenomena to avoid losing the specifics of the problems they face. The implications is that the problems that black people face in getting jobs as coaches and managers is deferred because the Asian problem is seen as far more pressing, because they are not even on the playing field.

On an institutional level, anti-racism has made league tables and the stages of promotion more public and pronounced: Sporting Equals Race Equality Charter standards, central government outputs on equity and equal opportunities policy documents focus on the outsider needing to change to be included. It has restricted the access of the outsider to seeking entry through the specific remits of equity targets, which map out very clear ways of travelling through the institutions without offering a direct route to the top. In this vein, Asians have become apparent as the new indicators of institutional change, their business mentality and shopkeeper heritage has made them more compatible with being inside the institutions as administrators rather than on the football field as performers. Cosmetically they are assumed to look more like white people and are less critical of their political past because their colonial history of oppression is much more limited in terms of time, and so are more accommodating and less rebellious regarding the culture of English soccer. More critically, despite the disregard for the complexity of their cultural history, anti-racism has reserved a place for them in a league where they can coexist within an assumed likeness to white men, but without the social and political power, despite their economic influence. It is a league where they can connect with the racism faced by black men because of their skin colour, and still have the luxury of being valued by white men, through a guilt based on a failure to integrate them on the field as players but realizing their economic and administrative value:

I am from an Asian background, more specifically from India, but I see myself as black politically rather than culturally. But the establishment seems to be showing signs of guilt at the Asian situation, showing recognition that there is shortage of Asian professionals, with the Asian population, most of which are mixed race, who are of a socialization that is not reflective of most Asian youth in this country. That is the recognition of the stage we are at. Now in terms of the Afro-Caribbean, they see a visible number on the field, so they think we are OK there. They don't consider the issues around management and coaching. As an industry they are ten and fifteen years behind practices in other industries. (Peter Smith)

Here in this comment we can begin to appreciate the difficulties in confronting an industry that cannot see how race is used as a tool to allocate positions. Peter identifies a crucial aspect of the anti-racism debate in football, in that Asians are not politically black, so they can fit into a range of spheres without having sold out. The overall effect is that the crude league table of race relation finds its foundation destroyed by Peter, by the possibility that 'Asian' is not a holistic and all embracing term as white people assume, and that Asian life cannot be simply compartmentalized. Their complexity outside of the sports context is determined by a range of associations. As Peter shows this emerging league table is not based on the diversity and flexibility of the individual, but a very powerful emotion called 'guilt'. It is a guilt in which black men are doing OK at the moment despite their absence in coaching and management, but there is a necessity to confront the shortage of Asians, to bring them in and place them on the public shelves of football.

Anti-racism then becomes a strategy in which institutions attempt to demonstrate that they are attending to the most in need, without really changing the democratic process that black players try to conquer, so creating an illusion we are actually moving towards a truly colour-blind industry, because the industry will accept anybody. The premier league, composed exclusively of white men does not change because this is about men competing as men without any reflection about their race. The league table outside these privileged white settings can change its composition dependent on which racial or national group is considered to be the most socially excluded.

More critically, the premier league of white men can influence and shape the role and purposes of Asian men and their restricted responsibility to always be the anti-racist experts, where all calls are directed towards them, thus centralizing the responses to racism. The accusation that Asians are only recruited because they are Asian, and because they more closely resemble the aspirations of white men, can be located and also contested in this statement by a leading Asian figure working at the Football Association:

I have never discussed my role in this organization as a member of an ethnic minority. Because of that there will be assumptions that are the area I should work on, with anti-racists trying to get more Asians into football. But there are a whole variety of other areas where I work, where no assumptions are made. It is also made more complicated that I am from a mixed race background. I think there are people with fixed ingrained attitudes about ethnic minorities who would have fewer difficulties with me because of my background than perhaps people from other communities. Many of my close friends have suffered a lot more in terms of racism in the work they are in. (Mark Hunt)

Mark Hunt is seen and celebrated as the highest profile Asian figure in the Football Association, having worked in the Communication Department. Firstly, Mark sees the misconception that what he looks like indicates what he will act like, his mixed-race background means he is easier to accept into whiteness. This notion of race and competence reminds us that the biological forms of racist assumptions made about black players in the field also take place in reference to Asian as good as administrators or good with money. Asian men inside football, look Asian and so are seen as most able to do anti-racist work, irrespective of all the other skills they may have. Mark expresses here the unwritten part of his job description, being seen as Asian, despite his diverse background, means he becomes the expert on Asian issues, based upon the fact that he is the only one. More importantly his presence is a reassurance to the organization that he is somebody they can 'deal with' who will not 'push the envelope' beyond the present capacity of the institutions to cope with evidence of racism in their setting.

Anti-racism, then, becomes a deeply emotional psychological test for firstly how individuals talk, look and work together, more crucially for how the outsider has to behave when restricted to being the anti-racist expert. The consequences for one's health are often never revealed, or allowed to be explored, because the real sacrifices involved in doing anti-racist work could have severely damaging implications for both the individual and the institutions. The implications of individuals having to represent a structure in which a generation of their people have been excluded, who then lose credability with the wider black community by promoting a reality of equality that is false to them. The damage to the institutions is that it functions through a pretence that by having Asian in the front window the death of Steven Lawrence has led to real changes in its democratic structures. It reminds the institutions that the price of silence is too high and the pressures too great for those given the responsibility of dealing with anti-racism, who can only reveal the acceptable face of racism inside football. So to be successful, in anti-racist work in football has tried to show concrete measurable outcomes, numbers, more people becoming qualified, but not taking the risk of recruiting the outsider who are unable to show an improvement in the performance of the organization in relation to their guidelines, and who breaks the illusion of real change:

There are definitely people in football that are more outward thinking who will definitely appoint Asian people. For example people in football especially in the Football in the community schemes realize that they can no longer operate in an environment that alienate ethnic minorities. They may need to appoint specific people in to work with specific communities. You will now see community coaches and administrators from ethnic minorities appointed for that specific reason. (Mark Hunt)

In this comment from Mark, anti-racism as an ethos is governed simply by having more black and Asian people inside football, whose competence is based on working with black and Asian people, a same-race matching in terms of their work allocation. The central challenge if more Asian people come into an environment in which they never contributed to the practices that have determined its culture is whether football changes and in what ways. Mark is far to diplomatic to expose the discrepancy between what people say and what they feel. He has had to play a far more sophisticated game, similar to the ones adopted by the black female manager in Chapter 4. His position between these three worlds, the Asian, the white and the black British, enables him to see more clearly the danger of forming leagues that forbid cross-cultural exchanges. Four divisions are emerging in which women are placed in the third, Asian men in the second and a group of black men stuck in the first division, just below a group of black players born abroad who are seen as foreign and are moving above them, but are still outside the elite premier commercial business league. The possibility of being transferred between these leagues is determined by the patronage of whiteness as explored in the last chapter. More specifically for the central message of this book black men who were once players are beginning to be banished to a league that no longer connects the worlds in which white men promote themselves.

The only league that seems to allow this merging of race and cultural groups is the powerless league of anti-racism, except when that league is structured by groups specifically for certain race associations. Consequently black- and Asian-only leagues, organizations and events are then seen as dangerous and too separatist to be considered as truly worthy of an anti-racist status, despite this approach being a response to years of alienation. Anti-racism inside soccer has really struggled with the formation of associations for black and Asian people, whilst other professions have come to terms with it, such as the police, the legal and the social work professions, and such bodies have a powerful position. Black players fear for their future in being associated with such groups. Ironically whilst white-only zones have existed historically without the same criticism, their power is not having to name themselves as white. Consequently to really engage in anti-racist work you have to be invited into the industry by these silent bodies of whiteness without being represented in their higher structures, or being represented at a cultural and political cost.

The issue of the cost of being in the organization, but not actually being represented, can be assessed through the experiences of Peter:

I have gauged that some assume that Ben would get a different hearing than I would get, but I think it is more complex than that, he is often seen as a football fan, well I am not easy to categorize, and his visible enthusiasm for his team is much more than me. He will get a hearing with a sort of white person, which is a grassroots football fan. If people are agreeing to see us they are making a mental adjustment, people pitch things at different levels, I am going as a coordinator, or they will appeal to Ben, it's very subtle but not very visible. (Peter Hunt interview 2000)

Peter talks about how individuals perceive his role compared to his then co-worker, Ben Smith, a white man. He developed a mental picture of this moment to be able to prepare himself for the way race operates in such an encounter and the potential difficulties he might face. He was able to see the complex implications of how anti-racism places individuals and attaches status, he had to try to get into the eyes and minds of the people who is working with. Although Peter was noted as the coordinator his credibility for running a campaign was tested not on race grounds, but because of football considerations first and foremost. The implications are that a love of football is the first priority before your allegiance to tackle racism may be respected by white people. This leads to a need to embrace the rhetoric of having to really be into football before your voice on dealing with anti-racism in relation to football is acknowledged. The irony is that white people can be laid back in their approach to tackle racism, but when black people are seen as laid back this is an inherent part of their character. It emphasizes the possibility, as raised by Ben Smith in an interview that 'I think that a white chairman may be more relaxed in talking to another white man', because white people, despite their anti-racist front, still find it difficult to relate to people who are not white. The consequence, in terms of anti-racist work in football, is that a negotiation is taking place in terms of who is considered the most suitable person to lead the debate, often determined again by the comfort zone of white men. More critically, even when the outsider has developed the correct performance and suitable language, this does not mean that we get any where nearer the racism that dictates the culture of institutions in football. What is occurring is that anti-racism is now enabling a completely new form of 'playing the white man' for both white men and Asians and a range of competing communities trying to be represented inside the structure of football.

The complexity of the performances of anti-racism as the new 'playing the white man' can be illustrated by a moment when I was on a coaching course. The tutor was talking about football diets and mentioned that, with more Asians coming into the game, the football diet may change. He points to an Asian student, assuming he would talk about Asian food, but he responded in a broad northern accent: 'I don't always like Asian food, me I like fish and chips.'

The comment situates an important but ironic position in the way this white male tutor presented the caring 'mode' of the anti-racist, inclusive and appealing to the positive changes Asians bring. It led to a response different from the one that he had expected with the Asian student embracing English football and dismissing any affinity to Asian food. This is a classic and important example of a disruption in anti-racist stereotypes and shows the implications when assumptions about the other are made and never checked, but are simply stated publicly. It has important implications for the limits of the cross-cultural exchanges that take place inside football, when approaches to anti-racism become fixed by how we define ourselves, or how others define us within a corresponding set of behaviours. The central problem with anti-racism as a form of classification is that it can lead to unexpected racist outcomes, it can leave us both exposed and embarrassed when the required set of behaviors or responses do not take place, and individuals are not allowed to behave beyond their roles. Firstly, because anti-racism in football leads to restricted avenues in which new communities can move into and operate, they know exactly where the escalator is going before they actually get on it, and it is usually the ground floor. Black players have not been able to get into a lift to move into positions as coaches and managers. Secondly, rather than opening new doors and becoming more socially inclusive, it can close the door and become more exclusive because it separates out the personnel and the structures who have responsibility for this work. It compartmentalizes anti-racism as a 'nine-to-five' work response and does not connect the attitudes that people bring into organizations as influencing their behaviour whilst they are in it.

Anti-racism thus creates an artificial, politically suspect environment in which individuals are fearful of saying the wrong thing, and being banished as racist for the rest of their lives. More crucially, the implications and outcomes of anti-racism are only activated by deciding whether to write and complain as an individual to an anti-racist organization and being involved in an investigation that can permanently damage the relationship between the parties. Such action can potentially distance the compliant from the fears of the exclusive white Premier club in accepting a trouble maker. This is a very real concern for black players who may need to depend on a white man for a reference, where many will be connected to the very same white man that they are complaining against.

Paradoxically the culprits have the option of redeeming themselves by restating their commitment to anti-racist work, by an apology, a show of 'show racism the red card' or the wearing of an anti-racist kick-it-out t-shirt or badge. These actions are irrelevant to the task of changing how their personal lives shape their approach to being 'nine-to-five' anti-racists, whilst they can be as racist as they like outside this time zone.

Anti-racism fails to explore how the idiosyncrasies of white men form the defining culture in institutions to enable them to retain their privilege of indifference and even hostility, in which they can decide when they want to be anti-racist, when it suits their needs. In this respect white men's feelings determine the pace of anti-racism and the types of structures in which anti-racism becomes a way of acting when their whiteness is threatened. Anti-racism, inclusion and exclusion are too crude to capture fully the range of experiences that black men may encounter and the settings in which they are assessed as being competent of being allowed in. The metaphor of the 'white man's country' used in the work of Miles (1982), in which he describes how the immigration policy of the 1970s and the 1980s was used to bring in desirable foreigners and exclude undesirable immigrants, is useful in understanding the role of anti-racism and social inclusion inside football.

At the higher levels of the game, as we have seen throughout this book, black players are overqualified, but still have not nurtured the types of persona or networks in which their entry into positions in coaching and management are guaranteed. Ironically they have witnessed a growth of white Europeans who have come into these positions ahead of them, as they are seen as civilizing the archaic English styles of coaching, enabling white men to communicate whilst they create a anxiety in white English men that they have come here to take their jobs. They have replaced black men as the new morel panic in English society. On occasions the emergence of the foreign manager has created a distraction, in that the delayed moment of black ex-players is due to their emergence as opposed to the long-standing issues of racism that black ex-players have confronted since the 1980s.

At the lower level of football, a whole range of funding has recently been created as football has got into bed with central government and crime prevention to use football to engage the hard to reach, as a model of social regeneration, to capacity build Asians and other 'minority groups' who are sold the dream of football promoting wider opportunities. This is where the whole notion of social inclusion and anti-racism becomes problematic, because the processes of social and political inclusion that are needed to move from the location of the outsider into the location of the institutions are never clearly articulated. Institutions inside football, as discussed throughout his book, coaching, management and administration appear more comfortable in achieving their race equality targets by using acceptable role models than paying radical attention to changing their structures. They cannot face the danger of removing pictures that reflect a heritage of a football empire built upon the undermining other racial groups who may request back what football has taken away from them. It is no longer guaranteed that white men will find an exclusive league table. They can no longer convince the outsider by their evangelistic rhetoric that they will only be accepted for entry if they comply with the rules:

No cause you can't. The reality is that you have to make sure black men and women are dealing with it in partnership . . . far rather, as a white middle age bloke work with you, and for you and me to agree rather than do it on my own. So you shouldn't trust me, so we should work together and deliver this together and stand shoulder to shoulder and show the next generation we are going to do this, this way. (Tom Harris)

This comment from a senior politician demonstrates the joint efforts needed to really confront racism inside football, in terms of whether white men can be trusted to allow people into their country, into all parts of their institutions at the higher levels. This notion of giving white people a hard time is contentious, because of the implications of the way white men determine the types of actions and words that can be used in the anti-racist debate. They control the people who can be critical of their cultural past and discrimination and the way in which the whole anti-racist struggle camouflages the manner in which black players are to denied entry by stating it will take time to change things.

This raises the problem of whether it is possible to stand together, black and white 'shoulder to shoulder', when our social and political worlds are so divorced, inside and outside of the context of sport – when the white man's shoulder is inside the structure and the others clearly outside. The message for the next generation is that the anti-racist approach in football has meant they will have to be careful how they can enter these sites of marginalized power, unclear about the games they need to play, the roles they will need to perform, and the permission they need to be truly promoted into the top structures of the game. Part of that permission can only be determined by investigating the barriers both individually and institution-ally for outside communities, from the perspective of the outsider, particularly at the ultimate level of black players moving into the white structures of coaching and management.

The Anti-racist Investigator

Restating the Pain: Those who Know It, Feel It
I feel that it is important to end this book by exploring the many roles adopted and conflicts faced to disentangle the cost of anti-racism to the lives of white, black and Asian people and the fundamental issues of representation inside structures of football. A term that is often used in the black community is 'those who know it, feel it', which suggests that those who feel the pain of racism are the ones who can talk about it most authentically.

I suggest that I have a real privilege as a black man to talk about racism and to rescue from the white voice the deception that only they can talk on behalf of all communities, because of an assumed distance as their unprivileged access to objectivity. It was my mission throughout this book to write and consider my authority to speak on behalf of one community of people, who may not see the implications of their actions, against another community, who feel the outcomes, but may feel powerless to do anything about it.

I consider I was placed in several conflicting positions in relation to these groups, not simply along race and cultural lines, but often by context and by dynamics. Consequently my own race cognizance and performance was tested when having to investigate and describe the powerless feelings of being unable to challenge racism in the institutions of soccer and to advocate on behalf of excluded groups at the moments in which these abuses take place. An inner despair often emerged of having to relive the abuse, by thinking about the abuse to analyse and write about the racist behaviours and words of the respondents. This meant reluctantly having to witness racism taking place by adopting a performance similar to the victims of this process, 'playing the white man', by being both subservient and compliant, to attempt to whiten my emotions, to be cold and distant. It meant trying to disconnect the pain of being a victim, which led to many sleepless nights, dreams of feeling attacked by white men, both politically and socially, and feelings that I had let myself, my family and community down, leading to displacing my anger into the wrong place because of the lack support from a community similar to that expressed by players who are so divorced from these processes. These important moments which may be regarded as being a martyr to the cause, having to be conciliatory towards white men, who may consider this book rhetorical, but these moments have become fundamental to trying to transcend being just another investigator, more specifically a black investigator who cannot disconnect the emotional pain from the risks of reporting racism.

The priority of the book through these emotional moments was the difficult task of moving away from a stark dualism and from always fixing the identities of the personnel as simply black, Asian or white, thus fixing my own identity as a black researcher. I also had to confront the additional problem of how race, masculinity and class, and the more underlying issues of sexuality operated in my personal practice in investigating racism inside football. In these cases I also had to 'play the white man', to negate the influences of my outside world, to perform a pretence to observe the individual experiences of both black and white men. Malcolm X's (1967) notion of the 'house nigger' articulates this de-political position of investigating anti-racism, to sell out to white men inside of the institutions of coaching and management by the use of their scientific methods, and to nullify the relationships between racism felt and experienced and the research agenda to investigate these issues. But it is this approach of apparent compliance, as a tool that opens up an industry to reveal its critical nature and provides a new dimension to an anti-racist investigator. 'Playing the white man' becomes an important research tool and performance that uncovers racism and personifies one of the public options of having to act to see racism taking place.

In this context the notion of the 'white mask', as a public research response to white men, similarly leads to internal reckoning as discussed in the lives of black managers in Chapter 4, through the development of a reflective methodological mirror. Like the black managers in Chapter 4, the mirror for the black researcher can again reflect outwards in terms of how you need to act in the interface with white men and inwards into the private world of the anti-racist investigator in terms of what this sacrifice means – preventing one's anger sabotaging the project. Consequently behind the 'white mask' complex cognitive processes were taking place, new strategies were emerging to engage a race pain killer, to be professional, to observe the deeper inadequacies and indifferences of men competing against men as forms of vulnerability. By the end of the project I could 'play the white man' by displacing my guilt in having to accept abuse as a legitimate enterprise of the research project, which helped ease and resolve my confusion about whether it was worth it, just to see the how institutional racism operates.

I did not want to neglect the very ordinary ways that men talk about their lives and the very ordinary ways in which they do their work as the foundation on which institutional cultures are built as the prerequisite to processes of inclusion and exclusion. The mission was to challenge the idea that racism is 'out there', and recognize that it is at the core of how white men colonialize the structures of soccer by the privilege of being able to operate within a comfort zone, to act white without consequences. Anti-racism, as a process of investigation, means going beyond one's comfort zone, it is the capacity of individuals to use their power to want to change, and to challenge and implement actions that individuals and institutions may not be emotionally prepared for. As a black researcher you define racism by how you see yourself implicated in processes of racism, by forcing yourself to look at how you may unconsciously contribute to the process of racism in terms of your beliefs and actions and how you impact upon the people or processes you are observing. This meant assessing, through my relationships with white men, the patterns of talk and action that makes them comprehensible, and the motives behind their resistance to declare their contributions towards racism in and outside the sporting context. It meant representing their voice by being sensitive, from a distance, to analyse their racism without showing my disapproval and value judgments, as Bourdeiu (1999) advocates, to make their racism intelligible but not acceptable. It meant having to attend to the life experiences of black men without collusion or being critical of their compliance, to hear and record their views, to accurately show that their views represented an important contribution to the diverseness of their situation.

True and meaningful anti-racism is to discover how white men and how black men perform together, and how this shapes the culture of the organization as an ongoing and changeable drama, in which the anti-racist investigator can be implicated by revealing his or her role and feelings. The task is then to enable individuals to see and examine the implications of their actions in the organizations in which they work. More crucially, it is to enable the anti-racist investigator to move away from a position of simply 'spying' to one of helping the actors to understand how their actions contribute towards institutional exclusion, whether 'unwitting' or not. It's important to consider my own feeling about how white men fall back on this notion of 'unwitting' as an escape clause in which they depersonalize their racism and remove the possibility of accountability. This can be compared to my anger at the treatment black men face, and their compliance needed to accommodate white racism as an 'unwitting form' in which they excuse and let white men off the hook, because racism as a form becomes untenable and not worth the risk of showing yourself up.

It is within the context of these struggles that I have tried to contribute to the need for new approaches to understand institutional racism, specifically in the institutions of soccer. My central point throughout this book has been the need to liberate ourselves from the constraints placed on us by the Macpherson's Report in relation trying to understand institutional racism, in the area of soccer. Macpherson (1999) has lacked a political impetus in defining and offering a clear strategy to tackle institutional racism. Although there have been changes in the anti-racist debate, these need to be measured in terms of representation and a real change in the culture.

If we are to use the notion of 'unwitting', to uncover both the white community and black men's roles in colluding with institutionalized racism, we need to place the ways these individuals act in institutions within a historical and cultural context. In terms of this book the task is to not polarize the individual and the institution but to connect their performances and narratives as two methods of describing and explaining the ways that individuals experiences being inside institutions, to assess the real powers of the Amendments to the 2000 Race Relation Act. This legislation was implemented after Macpherson, as a statutory approach to deal with racism in British society. It has been embraced in the context of sport in a very voluntary and cautious manner. It is now the time to make what has been conceived as voluntary acts of racism, without intent, seen and connected to statutory outcomes, where exclusion based on racism as a practice and attitudes is a legal and social injustice issue. The use of terms such as 'institutional racism', particularly in soccer, has encouraged individuals to disconnect their worlds, especially in linking 'racism' as individuals acting and talking in institutions, because of the fear of legal and moral redress. This fear has led to an approach to racism in institutions that has led simultaneously to either a blame culture, so the responsibility for racism becomes evasive, or disowned under the banner of 'personality conflicts' or 'that's not what I meant'.

In order to change this approach there is a need to invite individuals to work through a process of self-analysis in terms of how their different worlds link and contribute towards the cultures of the institutions in which they live and work. This means enabling individuals to understand their lives by using an approach to race and racism that is not punitive but instead encourages them to look at how they define themselves as parts of institutions and how they contribute to institutional exclusion inside soccer. The legal route should be the last resort. Unfortunately, the Sporting Equals Race Equality Charter, based on targets, has not penetrated the need to confront how race inequality actually operates inside football, to change its culture at the critical levels of coaching and management. It enables individuals to displace responsibility for racism on to the institution, by targets that reinforce the traditional belief that black ex-players are the victims, whilst white administrators are the perpetrators, or cannot see what they do.

Although it is now permissible to discuss other forms of racist abuse that take place on the training ground and in the relationships between black and white players on the field of play, this has not filtered into the political forms of inequality that travelled from outside the sport context into the institutions of coaching and management. Unfortunately the ideology of institutional racism and the fear that it instils in people who are afraid that they may be accused, has led to acts of racism in institutions becoming more implicit and hidden.

The information I gathered through my different roles within this book reflects the need for the institutions of coaching and management to address seriously how forms of whiteness operate and lead to the development of a culture of inclusion through familiarity and exclusion through fear of difference. The increased numbers of black players making the transition as coaches and managers, and the growth of black administrators, has been achieved through making sacrifices. The forms of deference demanded then contribute to new processes of institutional racism which are not recognized because of the mystic of the numbers game – having black personnel in positions means racism disappears. It is important then to explore the personal cost to white people in institutions who continue to deny and displace the fears that come with the threats of losing the privileges of being white. Perhaps, this is why the sense of resistance is so powerful, because ultimately this is a matter of relinquishing control, to give place to an outsider, in this move towards a multiracial representation in the institutions of soccer.

To conclude, I believe the present use of institutional racism and anti-racism has inhibited analysing how individual values and actions form whiteness that colonize the cultures and structures that operate inside of football and inside society. Until these connections have been established, white men will continue to enjoy the forms of privilege that have become naturalized in their relationships inside football, whilst black people will continue to struggle to fit into structures that cannot accommodate them unless they comply with the conditions in which the foundations of whiteness is built. More specifically I feel it important to register that the anti-racist investigator cannot simply sit back and observe, with some claim to objectivity. Their distance and failure to act is then intricately linked to the failure to disclose and leads to the perpetuation of institutional abuse. A simple analogy is that if you witness, the historical abuse of one race by another, similar to the adult abuse of the child, silence represents collusion, and failure to act does not represent protection. The movement from silence to talk and challenge is often provoked or inspired by emotional events, in this case death, the loss of a brother, the murder of another black man, all having been instrumental to the transition from the investigator to the political activist during the last thirteen years.

On 22 September 2003 I sat at a press conference at the Hilton Hotel in Islington with ten black retired players, fronted by the chief executive of the PFA, unprecedentedly talking openly about their experiences of discrimination and exclusion, which had previously been reserved and restricted to the research relationship.

This meeting and disclosure have been inspired, I selfishly and arrogantly announced, by a 13-year struggle, taking an activist approach to open up these institutions and show how racism operates, to allow white men to talk about the abuse of another race of people. It has forced the PFA into the first ever research into the needs of black players, inspired by years of canvassing by organizations like the Martin Shaw King Trust to go down this line. **The research has been instrumental in demonstrating that 36 per cent of black players believe institutional racism is a causal factor in their failure.** It has given the anti-racist investigator the capacity to assist the excluded to speak on their own behalf. It has enabled the anti-racist investigator to enlighten the excluders to attend to the need to get inside themselves and to change the processes of how they represent themselves in their structures and to put to them the strategies needed to change a history of neglecting the importance of truly multicultural institutional representation both politically and culturally. The Martin Shaw King Trust, named after my departed brother, supported my role in researching and writing this book and the pain of being placed on the outside, trying to get inside to change an exclusive culture that appealed to the power of white men.

During the last 13 years it has enabled me to obtain an UEFA A license badge and coach educator status, it has financed and supported the related PhD study on which this book has been based. More significantly it has enabled me to see the emotional and political costs of advocating on behalf of communities excluded on the basis of race, and the ways institutions use and steal ideas, marginalize when threaten and include when the project has some beneficial outcomes for themselves. It has enabled me to see and understand the games and strategies needed to persuade white people to take on the anti-racist struggle, by seducing them into seeing it was 'their idea', and that it will not lead to any severe cost to their personal lives in the 'nine-to-five' anti-racist role, and their private moments outside of this time limit. It has enabled me to see the types of black people they are prepared to promote as representing the face of anti-racism. This point can be illustrated during one moment when my colleague and I went to meeting with one of the funding agencies at the Football Association to discuss a proposal to hold an anti-racist conference during black history month. It's important here to describe the context: two 6 foot-tall-plus black men, one with long locks under his hat, whilst I had smaller locks, both dressed in tracksuits with the MSKT the Martin Shaw King Trust inscribed. After this meeting with a senior white female representative in an open-plan office, we shook hands, laughed and then walked out of the building. Some weeks later, discussing this proposal again with the white female, she disclosed that a senior white official had seen us leave the building and had casually remarked 'Have they come for money for guitar lesions?'

This comment is almost similar in its sentiment and political connotation to the comment used at the start of the book in relation to Darren who is told or requested to 'play the white man'. It has strong links to the words used by a white man in the bar during the coaching course in reference to locks, selling drugs and being a black Hitler. It is a fascinating revelation of the type of ideology held by white men whether on the playing field, or in the institutional setting of the Football Association – of their perception of black men's limitation attached to their social and political worlds both in and outside the world of soccer. Here the personification of Bob Marley and his twin are the only types of black men that white men can legitimately see as coming into their organization, unable to disrupt the norm of whiteness, that it is possible to be coherent, intellectual and strategic without looking and dressing like a white man. The inherent problem and contradiction faced in moving from the anti-racist investigator to the activist is how many personal changes are needed to assure white men that their institutions will not be populated by a generation of Bob Marley's singing and embracing his 'redemption song'.

On 28 October 2003 the trust held its second national conference facilitated and planned by those two black men, in conjunction with a variety of other football agencies, such as the Football Association, sitting shoulder to shoulder for the period of six hours to discuss issues of racism and joint partnership strategies needed to combat its evil forces. At about 4.30 all parties went to their separate homes, to their separate communities, and may not see each other again until the next conference or meeting. The league table of race which we have discussed in this chapter only assembled for one brief moment, and we will have to guess how these parties will translate into their personal lives the personal changes needed to make anti-racism a reality in both their public and private worlds.

Unfortunately any process of self-analysis and institutional change may depend on another black death or another atrocity against the civil rights of black people outside of soccer with clear ramifications for the lives of people inside the world of football. Whilst we wait for white men to move their offside racism onside, through being challenged, or being motivated through moral guilt, the anti-racist investigator runs the risk of being alienated by having to accept strategies determined by white people who set the pace of change in relation to their own needs.

The real indication of change is when anti-racism becomes a metaphor of a bygone age, when the race constructions of league tables are dismantled and we can engage in new languages and approaches that operate not from moral guilt but based upon personal affinity with the issues that transcend the danger of the demarcation of race. The marker of true anti-racism is when we are allowed to forget how our race constrains and control and when we remove the power of those who impose the need to play the white man to seek acceptance and representation inside English football.

The crucial problem in terms of sport is to remove the image articulated throughout this book that the mind and the body are two entities, and to remove the stereotypes resonating in the lives of black people from their families, through their schooling into the world of football.

Often we are told that slavery has ended, and it is unfair to set up the white man as the slave master and the black man as the slave, which is too simplistic. In fact the echoes of this period contributed to one of the most important political rationales concerning how sport is an important hegemonic relationship between society and racism. The answer to many of these questions of how these themes link can only be revealed through the black experience, which holds a very important key in translating how sport articulates wider power relationships in English society. The themes that operate in sport are very similar, as my brother Trevor tells me from his work in mental heath: the themes of not knowing white men's private thoughts and the risk of challenging their behaviour especially if one is seeking promotion.

We are also beginning to see the role white women play in acting out the pressures of a culture determined by white men, and seeing the power they have over groups who are not white despite their masculinity, and beginning to accept that we are always considering the cost of what it means to play the white man wherever we are, and that in many situations it may have a positive effect if it opens a door.

What is required is a completely new perspective to what it means to 'play the black man' in English society and English football, especially if white men are to develop a level of empathy to give up their privileges and to begin to move towards equity based upon some level of insight rather than a moral guilt. This removes the need for a 'white mask' and not having to divide our worlds between the white one and the black one, but to realize the complex cross-cultural changes that are not allowed to operate because of the discomfort zones of being different. It raises the possibility of races working across rigid leagues to dismantle the processes of anti-racism that keep them separate and unable to work in true partnership. For the anti-racist investigator it raises the possibility of disposing of this title and label and being accepted on equal terms with white men who have the privilege of talking without any accountability for their whiteness and who are never asked to 'play the black man' and of being more authentic on their approach to understanding institutionalized racism in football. The real challenge for football in the twenty-first century in not simply the problem of the colour line as suggested in the work of

Du Bois, but the problem of how we address the problem of colour differences as the premise on which white men control the entry points into coaching and management. It is the challenge of not always seeing colour as the problem for the entry of black and Asian people, but what colour means for white people to give up their power and to remove the conditions on which the others have to 'play the white man' to be accepted. It is the real challenge for black players to move into jobs as coaches and managers without reference to the demarcation of race, and to realize, unfortunately, that we are still prisoners to a system in which how we look determines how we act and the places in institutions where we are allowed to go. The danger is that a kind of *apartheid* is still present inside British society. Irrespective of communities living closer together this *apartheid* is still reflected in the structures of English society where there are very few black managers at the very top. In the context of English soccer this is also apparent in the lack of representation of black and Asian people inside the structures of the game and the lack of consideration of what it may take to put to bed the legacy of colonialism and release the powers that have been transferred into sport where white men have privileges, but do not realize that there is no honour in a British empire that cannot apologize and repay what it has stolen through the context of football. Until this culture of reflection, of linking what happens in football to the outside world, is achieved, the notion of the level playing field will be used as convenient excuse. For white men truly to level out the field is to return to the plantation field in which many of their attitudes and much of their heritage are formed, the stereotype of the black body and intelligence. Until this process of dismantling whiteness, it power and privilege takes place, it will not be possible to escape having to 'play the white man' to find a place inside the structures of English soccer.

Bibliography

Ashe, A. (1993) *A Hard Road to Glory – History of the African-American Athlete, 1619–1918*, New York: Rockefeller Centre.

Ashe, A. (1993) *A Memoir: A Day of Grace*, London: Heinemann.

Atkinson, R. (1998) *Big Ron: A Different Ball Game. A Football Memoir by Ron Atkinson*, London: Andre Deutsch.

Back, L., Crabbe, T. and Solomos, J. (2001) *The Changing Face of Football. Racism, Identity and Multiculture in the English Game*, London: Berg.

Bains, J. (1996) *Asians Can't Play Football*, Birmingham: D-Zine

Bains, J. and Patel, R. (1996) *Asians Can't Play Football*, Birmingham: Asian Social Development Agency.

Bains, J. and Sanjiev, J. (1998*) Corner Flags and Corner Shops. The Asian Football Experience*, London: Victor Gollancz.

Barnes, J. (1999) *John Barnes: The Autobiography*, London: Headline.

Basso (1979) *Portraits of the Whiteman: Linguistic Play and Cultural Symbols among the Western Apache*, Cambridge: Cambridge University Press.

Bourdieu, P. (1999) *The Weight of the World*, Cambridge: Polity Press.

Bradbury, S. (2001) *The New Ethnic Communities. A Survey of Professional Football Clubs on Issues of Community, Ethnicity and Social Inclusion*, Leicester: University of.

Carrington, B. (1986) *Social Mobility.*

Carrington, B. and McDonald, I. (2001*) 'Race', Sport and British Society*, London and New York: Routledge.

Cashmore, E. (1982) *Black Sportsmen*, London and New York: Routledge & Kegan Paul.

Charlton, J. (1996) *The Autobiography*, London: Corgi Books.

Clough, J. (1994) *The Autobiography*, London: Patridge Press.

Cole, A. (1999) *The Autobiography. Andy Cole*, London: Manchester United Books.

Dalglish, K. (1996) *My Autobiography*, London: Hodder & Stoughton.

Davidson, S. (1996) 'What has been the Contribution of Social Policy to the Assessment Process of Black Children.' *A Study of one Local Authority' Department of Government: Brunel University*, Unpublished papers.

Du Bois, W. D. (1903) *Souls of a Black Folk*, New York: Dover Publications.

Dunning, E., Murphy, P. and Williams, J. (1988) *The Roots of Football Hooliganism: An Historical and Sociological Study*, London: Routledge.

Earle, R. and Davies, D. (1998) *One Love. The Story of Jamaica's Reggae Boyz and the 1998 World Cup*, London: Andre Deutsch.

Entine, J. (2000) *Why Black Athletes Dominate Sports: And Why We're Afraid To Talk About It*, New York: Public Affairs.

Fanon, F. (1967) *Black Skin, White Mask*, London: Pluto Press.

Ferdinand, L. (1997) *Sir Les: The Autobiography of Les Ferdinand*, London: Hodder Headline.

Fleming, S. (1995) *Home and Away: Sport and South Asian Male Youth*, Aldershot: Avebury Publications.

Fisher Fishkin, S. (1996) 'Interrogating "Whiteness" Complicating "Blackness" Remapping American Culture'. *American Quarterly*, 47 (3): 428–65

Football Task Force (1998) *Eliminating Racism from Football: A Report by the Football Task Force Submitted to the Minister for Sport*, London: The Football Task Force.

Frankenberg, R. (1993) *White Women, Race Matters. The Social Construction of Whiteness*, New York and London: Routledge.

Gilroy, P. (1987) *There Ain't No Black in the Union Jack: The Cultural Politics of Race and Nation*, London: Hutchinson.

Gilroy, P. (1993*) The Black Atlantic: Modernity and Double Consciousness*, London and New York: Verso.

Gilroy, P. (2000*) Between Camps. Nations, Cultures and the Allure of Race*, London and New York: The Penguin Press.

Glanvill, R. (1996) *The Wright Stuff*, London: Virgin.

Goffman, E. (1956) *The Presentation of Self*, London: Penguin.

Graham, G. (1996) *The Glory and the Grief*, London: Andre Deutch.

Griffin, J. (1960) *Black Like Me*, New York: Penguin.

Gullit, R. (1997) *My Autobiography*, London: Century.

Haley, A. (1965) *The Autobiography of Malcolm X*, New York: Penguin.

Hamilton, A. (1982) *Black Pearls of Soccer*, London: Harrap.

Hamilton, A. and Hinds, E. (1999) *Black Pearls: The A-Z of Black Footballers in the English Game*, London: Hansib.

Hargreaves, J. (1986) *Sport, Power and Culture. A Social and Historical Analysis of Popular Sport in Britain*, Oxford: Polity Press.

Hoberman, J. (1997) *Darwins Athletes: How Sport Damaged Black America and Preserved the Myth of Race*, Boston: Hougton Mifflin.

hooks, b. (1991) *Black Looks Race and Representation*, Boston: South End Press.

Hill, D. (1989) *Out of his Skin: The John Barnes Phenomenon*, London: Faber & Faber.

James, C. L. R. (1967) (1994) *Beyond a Boundary*, London: Serpent's Tail.

Jarvie, G. (1991) *Sport Racism and Ethnicity*, London, New York, Philadelphia: Falmer Press.

Kane, M. (1971) 'An Assessment of Black is Best London'. *Sport Illustrated Magazine*, 72–83.

Kelly, G. (1999) *Sweet F.A. A Fascinating Insight into Football's Corridor of Power*, London: Collins Willow.

Kovell, J. (1988) *White Racism. A Psychohistory*, Exeter: Short Run Press Ltd.

Macpherson, Sir W. (1999) *The Stephen Lawrence Enquiry. The Report of an Inquiry by Sir William Macpherson of Cluny*, London: CRE.

Maguire, J. (1991) 'Sport, Racism and British Society. A Sociological Study of Elite Male. Afro/Caribbean, Soccer and Rugby Union Players', in Jarvie, G. (ed.) *Sport, Racism and Ethnicity*, London: Fulmer Press.

McGuire, B. and Collins, D. (1998) 'Sport, Ethnicity and Racism: the Experience of Asian Heritage Boys'. *Sport, Education and Society*, 1 (3): 79–88.

Merill, J. Melnick. (1988) 'Race Segregation by Playing Position in the English Football League: Some Preliminary Observations'. *Journal of Sport and Social Issues*, 12 (2): 122–3.

Miles, R. (1982) *White Man's Country*, London: Routledge.

Miles, R. (1993) *Racism After 'Race Relations'*, London and New York: Routledge.

Portelli, A. (1991) *The Death of Luigi Trastulli and Other Studies. Form and Meaning Oral History*, Albany: State University of New York Press.

Roediger, D. (1991) *The Wage of Whiteness*, London: Verso.

Rodney, W. (1982) *How Europe Underdeveloped Africa*, Washington DC: Howard University Press.

Shropshire, K. L. (1996) 'Sports Agents, Role Models and Race-Consciousness'. *Marquette Sports Law Journal*, 6 (2): 267–287.

Szymanski, S. (1993) 'A Market Test for Discrimination in the English Professional Soccer League'. *Journal of Political Economy*, 108 (3): 597–68.

Taylor, I. (1982) 'On Sport Violence Question; Soccer Hooliganism Revisted' in Hargreaves, J. (eds) *Sport, Culture and Ideology*, London: Routledge.

Utchay, T. K. (1975) White-Manning in West Africa', in Nancy, N. (ed.) *Negro Anthology*, New York: Frederick Ungar.

Vasili, P. (1998) *The First Black Footballers. Arthur Wharton 1865–1930. An absence of Memory*, London: Frank Cass.

Vasili, P. (2000) *Colouring Over the White Line. The History of Black Footballers in Britain*, Edinburgh and London: Mainstream Publishing.

Venables, T. (1995) *The Autobiography*, London: Headline.

Victor, P. (1993) ' Did Slavery Help put Blacks on Top in Sport?' *Sunday Times*.

Ware, V. and Back, L. (2001) *Out of Whiteness Colour, Politics And Culture*, Chicago: The University of Chicago Press.

Welsing, C. (1991) *The Isis Papers*, Chicago: Third World Press.

Wiggins, D. K. (1991) 'Great Speed but Little Stamina. The Historical Debate over the Athletic Superiority'. *Journal of Sport History*, 16 (3): 158–189.

Williams, J. (1985) *'Institutional Racism'*: New Orthodoxy, Old Ideas.

Williams, J. (1991) *Lick my Books – Racism in English Soccer*, Leicester: Department of Sociology, University of Leicester.

Williams, J. (1994) ' "Rangers is a Black Club", "Race" Identity and Local Football in England', in Giulianotti, R. and Williams, J. (eds) *Games without Frontiers*, Aldershot: Avebury.

Williams, J. P., Dunning, E.G. and Murphy J. (1984) 'Come On You Whites', *New Society*, 24 May 1984.

Woolnough, B. (1983) *'Black Magic' England's Black Footballers*, London: Pelham.

Wood, E. R. and Carrington, L.B. (1982) 'School, Sport and Black Athletics', *Physical Education Review*, 5 (2): 131–7.

Wright, I. (1972) *The Explosive Autobiography of Ian Wright*, London: HarperCollins.

Index

ability, 70, 71–2, 80
abuse, 16, 103
  football crowds, 19–20, 22–3
  under slavery, 17, 18
  witnessing and accepting, 124–5,
    127
academic work (coaching courses), *see*
  classroom-based work
acceptance
  of Asians, 116
  of black players, 20–1, 23, 24, 70,
    81
  criteria, 46
  of difference, 73
  processes of, 67–8
accountability, lack of, 67, 70
accusations of racism, 91–2, 101, 121,
  126
activism, inspiration for, 127–8
administrators
  Asians, 116
  interview samples, 7
  racial breakdown, 6
advocacy, 128
Africa, 72–3
alienation, 37–8
  self-, 67
allegiance, 60
American sport, 13
Anderson, Viv, 77–8
Andrews, Michael, 82

anti-racism, 113, 114, 116–21
  and Asians, 118
  control of debate, 123
  spokesmen, 120
  true, 125, 129–30
apartheid, 131
appearance, 36, 101, 128–9
  dreadlocks, 25, 103
  dress codes, 30–1
appointment, *see* recruitment
  processes
Ash, A., 13
Asian and black associations, 119
Asians
  acceptability, 116–18
  perception of, 120
  players and ex-players, 2, 28,
    114–15
assault, 39
assessment (coaching courses), 30,
  33–5, 44–5
assimilation, 14
  Asians, 116–17
  through performance of whiteness,
    2
associations, black and Asian,
  119
assumptions, racist, 106, 118
  see also stereotypes
Atkinson, Ron, 11, 97
authority figures, white, 22

Gayle, Howard, 96
gaze, black, 44
Gilroy, P., 14, 113–14
Glanvill, R., 11
Goffman, E., 3, 29, 41
grassroots level (of football), 47
guilt, white male, 85–6, 103–5, 111
  concerning Asians, 117
Gullit, Ruud, 12, 83–4

Hamilton, A., 15
Hargreaves, J., 13
Harris, Ian, 24, 56–7, 69
Harris, Tom, 122
hegemony, sport and society, 13, 130
heritage
  black players, 25
  National Sports Centre, 30
hierarchy, 45
  racialized, 58
Hill, D., 11
Hill, Ricky, 78
Hill, Terry, 105–6
Hoberman, J., 12–13
Hoey, Kate, 108
hooks, b., 14
hostility, 100–1
'house niggers' and 'field niggers', 5,
  18, 75–6, 81–3
humour, *see* comments and jokes,
  racist; parody
Hunt, Mark, 117–19
Hunt, Peter, 120

identity, 11, 31, 113–14
  black, 59–60, 89
  coaches, 57–8, 63–4, 70
  managers, 88
  public and private, 85
  racial, 3, 14
  white, 98–9

image, 60
  mind and body, 130
  of whiteness, 31
inclusion, 45–6, 107, 127
  anti-racism, 121
  white men, 42
industry, football, 26–8
inferiority, sense of, 69
influence, economic and political, 77
institutional culture, *see* culture
institutional racism, *see* racism
institutions, 126
  of management, 75, 77
intelligibility
  racism, 44–5, 125
  whiteness, 111
interception, 72
internalization, 12–13
international level of football, 22–3
interviews, 73–4, 99–100
  dynamics, 101–2
  table of samples, 7
investigator, anti-racist, 123–5, 127,
  128, 130
isolation, black students, 32

Jackson, Les, 51, 62–3
Jackson, Tony, 63–4
James, C., 13–14
Jenkins, Marlon, 33–5
jokes, racist, *see* comments and jokes,
  racist
Jones, Frank, 98, 108
judgement
  black players and ex-players, 21–2,
    84–6
  suspension of, 125

Kamara, Chris, 92
Kane, M., 9
Kelly, G., 12

Ouseley, Herman, 95
outside football, *see* world outside
   football
outsider, the, 116, 118, 122–3

pain, of racism, 123–4
Parker, Colin, 15–16, 21
parody, 5, 35–6, 37, 42–3
   see also comments and jokes, racist
participant observation, 7–8, 37–9,
   43–4, 124
partnership, 122–3
pathologization
   black people, 5–6, 9, 12, 13, 16, 91
   whiteness, 111
perception
   of Asians, 120
   of black men, 84–5, 92–3, 129
   of football, 17
   of whiteness, 95
performance, 4, 41–2, 72, 76
   of anti-racism, 120
   black managers, 86
   participant observation, 124
   ritualized, 33, 34
   of whiteness, 1–3
perspective, of black players and
   ex-players, 78–9, 81–2
plantation field (metaphor), 18
players and ex-players
   Asian, 2, 28, 114–15
   black, 1–2, 21–2, 54–61, 67–86
      passim, 115
      exclusion, 25–6, 29, 45–6, 76–7,
         82–3, 128
      experiences, 5–6, 13, 15–16,
         75–6
   narratives, 49–50, 61
   professional
      racial breakdown, 6
   white, 23–4, 50–4, 61–6

playing positions, 10, 116
'playing the black man', 130
'playing the white man', 1, 5, 77, 120,
   124–5, 131
   see also strategies; 'white mask'
political correctness, 60, 71, 91–2
Portelli, A., 5, 49
post-colonialism, *see* colonialism
power
   of black ex-players, 80
   dynamics, 22, 28
   evasiveness, 49, 51, 61
   formations, 109–10
   of white men, 21, 24–5, 36–7, 56,
      61, 81–2, 95–8
   of whiteness, 13, 14
powerlessness, 55–6
Premier League, 6
pressures, psychological, 20–1, 80,
   82
private life, *see* worlds, public and
   private
privilege, of whiteness, 95–8, 104,
   109, 121–2
processes
   acceptance, 67–8
   change, 129
   racism, 18, 20, 125
   whiteness, 95–6
Professional Footballers' Association,
   6, 107, 128
profile, high
   black players, 79–82
psychology
   in football, 21–2
   of racism, 17
psychotic states
   whiteness, 111
public life, *see* worlds, public and
   private
puppets (metaphor), 76, 78